INTIMATE MOMENTS WITH GOD

To - Nellie S Tarabee
From - The Wm. Green Family
Date - Nov. 22. 2006

Compiled by

Linda Evans Shepherd

and

Eva Marie Everson

Honor Books

Scripture quotations marked AMP are taken from *The Amplified Bible. Old Testament* copyright © 1965, 1987 by Zondervan Corporation, Grand Rapids, Michigan. *New Testament* copyright © 1958, 1987 by the Lockman Foundation, La Habra, California. Used by permission.

Scripture quotations marked KJV are taken from the *King James Version* of the Bible.

Verses marked TLB are taken from *The Living Bible* © 1971. Used by permission of Tyndale House Publishers, Inc., Wheaton, Illinois 60189. All rights reserved.

Scripture quotations marked THE MESSAGE are taken from *The Message*, copyright © by Eugene H. Peterson, 1993, 1994, 1995, 1996. Used by permission of NavPress Publishing Group.

Scripture quotations marked NASB are taken from the *New American Standard Bible*. Copyright © The Lockman Foundation 1960, 1962, 1963, 1968, 1971, 1972, 1973, 1975, 1977, 1996. Used by permission.

Scripture quotations marked NET are taken from the *NET (New English Translation) Bible*. Copyright © 1997-2001 by Biblical Studies Press, L. L. C., and the authors. All rights reserved.

Scripture quotations marked NIV are taken from the *Holy Bible, New International Version®*. NIV®. Copyright © 1973, 1978, 1984 by International Bible Society. Used by permission of Zondervan Publishing House. All rights reserved.

Scripture quotations marked RSV are taken from *The Holy Bible Revised Standard Version*. Copyright © 1946, 1952. Used by permission of the Division of Christian Education of the National Council of Churches of Christ in the United States of America. All rights reserved.

Scripture quotations marked NKJV are taken from *The New King James Version*. Copyright © 1979, 1980, 1982, Thomas Nelson, Inc.

Scripture quotations marked BWE are taken from *The Jesus Book, The Bible in Worldwide English, New Testament*. Copyright © 1969, 1971, 1996, 1998, SOON Educational Publications. Used by permission. All rights reserved.

07 06 05 04 03 10 9 8 7 6 5 4 3 2 1

Intimate Moments with God

ISBN 1-56292-498-2

Published by Honor Books

An Imprint of Cook Communications Ministries

4050 Lee Vance View

Colorado Springs, Colorado 89018

Introduction

Want to see the heart of God? Want to know what God really thinks about the struggles and joys in your life? Your favorite Bible verse may tell you more than you realize. The Scriptures are more than just words written on scrolls and passed down throughout the generations. Amid heartbreaking agonies and heart-lifting joys, they provide comfort, encouragement, and joy. However, they also give us a picture of the heart of God. No wonder they have survived for thousands of years! No wonder the Bible is the number-one, best-selling book of all time!

Many of us have discovered a single scripture that speaks directly to our need and we capture it in our hearts allowing it to speak to us throughout our lives. That scripture speaks volumes about us and about God's work in us. For example, during a book signing I sat behind a counter, teetering on the edge of a barstool, signing one book after the other. As is my custom, I greeted each "fan," chatting briefly. In the middle of the flow of people and books, a man stepped up and said, "I'd like to ask you something personal."

My pen stopped in its strokes and I looked him in the eyes. "Yes?"

"What is your favorite scripture?"

I answered the question, followed by telling him why. After all, *that* question just demands a "why." The man smiled. I finished signing his book and he walked away.

It was some time later that I realized what he had done. He'd gotten to know more about *me* . . . the person—not just the *author* or the *speaker*. What a blessing for me!

I remember the funeral of my neighbor's twenty-year-old daughter like it was yesterday. The new pastor of their church hadn't had the opportunity to get to know Laura, who'd been killed in an auto accident. However, to aid him in preaching the funeral, her parents handed him Laura's Bible. There were notes jotted in the margins, favorite passages highlighted and underlined. At the funeral, he spoke as though he'd known Laura all her short life. Her love for Scripture revealed her life and the call she had fulfilled.

Intimate Moments with God captures how just one scripture spoken by God can change our lives and reveal God's hand. I trust you will see the heart of God revealed to the women who share a glimpse of their life-changing encounters with God. May you be encouraged by their examples to invite Him to come near and make His words come alive in your life as well.

Eva Marie Everson
Right to Heart Board Member
Advanced Writers & Speakers Association

Contents

Walk, Don't Run

Jill Rigby

I run in the path of your commands,
for you have set my heart free.
Psalm 119:32 NIV

Do you run all day? Let's see—from the bed to the carpool to the grocery to the laundry to the kitchen to the carpool and back to bed? From the bed to the office to the grocery store to the bank to the cleaners to lunch to the house to the gym and to bed again?

Several years ago, I became tired of running in the path I had chosen for my life. I felt I was living in bondage. I had ceased "being." I was a programmed machine, without a heart, whose switch was turned on at 5 A.M. and turned off at 10 P.M. I decided it was time to see if the path I was running was God's plan for me, so I cleared my calendar for the next month. I literally erased every entry and laid it on the kitchen counter and said to the Lord, "I am Yours and my days belong to You. I want to have a heart again. Will You fill my days with Your agenda?"

I began receiving phone calls canceling events. Plans were changed at the last minute that had been in place for months. New opportunities unfolded that I had never considered. Suddenly, I found time to "be" again. My family appreciated the overflow of love that came from the new schedule. I began looking forward to each day rather than dreading the next day's "to do list."

The week after the revelation in my kitchen, my ladies' Bible group began a study of Psalm 119. Imagine my delight when I reached verse 32! I have claimed this verse as a prayer of gratitude ever since.

I'm still running, but now I'm running in the path of God's commands for my life. I have the freedom to be who He created me to be. Are you held in bondage to your schedule? Give your calendar back to the Lord and He will set your heart free.

O Lord, enable me to run with great joy in the path You have prepared for me. Thank You for setting my heart free. I love You and I praise You, Lord.

Jill Rigby has a passion for drawing women into the loving arms of our Heavenly Father when disappointments threaten to destroy their faith. She is the author of *Manners of the Heart.*

Immunization

Jennie Afman Dimkoff

"Never will I leave you; never will I forsake you."

Hebrews 13:5 NIV

My husband and I waited nine years to have children. During that time, our two Siamese cats were our babies. There was just one problem. They needed immunizations, and I couldn't bear the thought. (As a five-year-old, I had been treated for rheumatic fever and endured regular, painful injections. I *hated* shots.)

I tucked both cats inside an old picnic basket and headed to the clinic. Upon arriving, I handed the basket to the veterinarian and then opted to wait outside until the nasty deed was done.

The door opened, a nurse handed me the basket, and we went home.

Years later, I had children and *they* needed immunizations! At our first appointment I learned that I was not allowed to hand the infant carrier to the nurse and leave! I actually had to hold my baby while the nurse gave my daughter the injection. Her little face turned red, and clutching my hair in her tiny fist, she wailed at me in shock and pain. I cried too.

Nonetheless, as my children grew (and although it grieved me), I took them for every shot required. Why? Because I loved them so much, and even I, with my limited medical knowledge, understood that somehow the temporary discomfort they endured would prepare them for the future.

That experience has helped me understand a little better how God, in His infinite love for me, has allowed some painful experiences in my life. Things I wouldn't have chosen. Things I didn't understand. But, while I was enduring the pain, shock, or despair, God was always right there, holding me as lovingly as I held my babies. And He was whispering, "I'm here, child, and I'll never leave you or forsake you. Trust Me."

O Father, when I feel frightened or alone, help me to remember that You love me, You will never abandon me, and that You can work even painful things together for good in my life.

Jennie Afman Dimkoff is a motivational speaker, gifted storyteller, trainer, and the author of *Night Whispers, Bedtime Bible Stories for Women*. She is the president of Story Line Ministries, Inc.

His Plans Are Best

Rebecca Barlow Jordan

We know that in all things God works for the good of those who love him, who have been called according to his purpose.
Romans 8:28 NIV

As my teenage sweetheart and I flew past the stop sign and into the intersection without stopping, I remember looking up and seeing two bright mammoth eyes speeding toward us. In a split second, a pickup truck hit us broadside, just behind Larry on the driver's side. We spun like an amusement park ride and landed in a ditch by the side of the road. The impact left the door on Larry's shiny, black Plymouth Fury badly crushed and inoperable.

We later learned that except for a few punctures that needed stitches and some other light cuts and bruises, we all fared well. Some unseen angels must have been at work that night. The highway patrolman who investigated the accident just shook his head as he looked at the twisted wreckage. "Son, I hope you realize you could have all been killed."

The wreck totaled Larry's car and left us shaken, and we pondered what good God would possibly bring from this ordeal. The car collision that almost had demolished our dreams of sharing life together instead prompted a new dream.

A few months later Larry surprised me with the question, "How do you feel about being a preacher's wife?" Through those circumstances, Larry had taken a new look at the life God had spared and began to sense God calling him to full-time ministry, and within a few years, this preacher's daughter became a preacher's wife. God had used a car accident to rearrange both of our lives—His way.

Thirty-six years later, He is still working things out for our good.

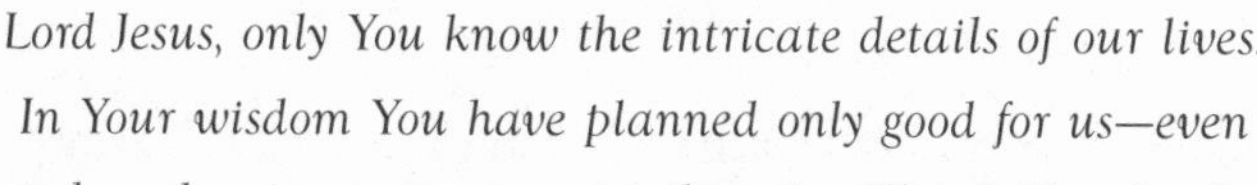

Lord Jesus, only You know the intricate details of our lives. In Your wisdom You have planned only good for us—even when the circumstances say otherwise. Thank You, Lord.

Rebecca Barlow Jordan, a speaker and best-selling author, has shared God's goodness in over 1600 inspirational works and numerous books, including *At Home in My Heart* and *Daily in Your Presence.*

For His Own Sake

Kathy Collard Miller

"I, even I, am the one who wipes out your transgressions for My own sake, and I will not remember your sins."
Isaiah 43:25 NASB

"Oh, God, please forgive me," I prayed again, "but how can You when I'm the worst of all sinners! I physically abused my own daughter!"

I tried to believe God could forgive me but it seemed impossible. Even though I'd seen God's wonderful power change me into a patient, loving mother, my previous sin seemed unforgivable.

Then one day as I flipped through my Bible, something caused me to pause and stare at Isaiah 43:25. I'd never noticed it before. I read it out loud slowly and then prayed, "Oh, Father, I know You want to wipe out my sin, but are You saying that You want to forgive me for *Your* benefit?"

Tears formed in the corners of my eyes and the page blurred. I tried to mull over the significance of that phrase: "*for My own sake.*" I'd always thought of forgiveness as something for my benefit, but here it said that God wanted to forgive me—for *His* benefit, too. I then realized that if I didn't accept His forgiveness, He couldn't have fellowship with me. *That's His benefit!*

Now the tears cascaded down my cheeks in relief and surrender. *God wants my fellowship! I'm blocking that by not accepting His forgiveness! He loves me that much!*

Over the next days and weeks, the pain of my sin diminished as I allowed God's forgiveness to wash over me. My fellowship with God increased, and I rejoiced that I could give God a benefit! Today, many years later, the pain of my sin is completely gone, and my daughter and I have a fabulous relationship. My ministry began out of the sin that seemed too grievous. Now I can assure others who feel they can never be forgiven that God wants to forgive them *for His benefit!*

Heavenly Father, to think You gain from forgiving me is difficult to understand; but I ask You to forgive me of my sin. Help me know You delight in our relationship. Amen.

Kathy Collard Miller is the author of over forty-five books, including *Princess to Princess*, and is a popular women's conference speaker.

His Plan, His Purpose, My Privilege

Pamela Christian

"If you repent, I will restore you that you may serve me; if you utter worthy, not worthless, words, you will be my spokesman. Let this people turn to you, but you must not turn to them."

Jeremiah 15:19 NIV

"Lord, please don't put me out to pasture; I'm only in my early forties!" I loved teaching the women's Bible study. "Please show me what I can do now that we've moved."

I wiped away tears as I prayed. The phone rang, startling me as I rose. It was a former classmate calling to see if I'd be their retreat speaker. "You have no idea of the timing of your call," I said. "I'll pray about it."

Opening the mailbox a day later, I recognized the handwriting of my dear friend June. She enclosed a brochure for a seminar that trains speakers for retreats and conferences. June sent along a note insisting that I attend, stating she would pay my registration.

With all the fears of a first-day college student, I attended the three-day seminar. My nerves and episodes of panic got the better of me and I almost quit, but I managed to complete my final assignment. Betty Southard, my small-group instructor, took me aside. "What in the world is the matter with you, Pam? You have what it takes. Why did you almost give up on the class?" Embarrassed, the tears started to flow. *I did it! With God's help, I did it!*

The next morning in the comfort of my robe and slippers, I prayed, "But, Lord, this is way beyond anything I've done. I need to know if You want me to do this." Interrupted by the ringing of the phone, I answered and heard my sister say that she'd been praying for me and felt strongly about sharing Jeremiah 15:19 with me. I finally realized that God wanted me to repent from doubting what He could do with a willing vessel. More amazed than anyone, I have found myself to be a spokesman for God and the founder of Pamela Christian Ministries.

Almighty God, I bow low to the reality of what You've done for me. I long to live my life in such a way that You are glorified, that it is readily apparent that You are my Lord. Help me to live faithfully to Your Word for me from Jeremiah 15:19. Amen.

Pamela Christian is a keynote speaker for retreats and conferences, coast to coast.

Angels Unaware

Louise Tucker Jones

He will command his angels concerning
you to guard you in all your ways.
Psalm 91:11 NIV

I knew that Jay could never make up the things he told me—a bright angel stood at his door every night. I have always known about angels, but they didn't become a reality in my life until my youngest son, who has Down's syndrome and progressive heart disease, told me about seeing an angel at his doorway. That caused me to take notice. Yes, I believed in angels but I certainly had never seen one.

Some months later, when Jay's health required him to begin to sleep with oxygen, he was scared and asked me to pray for angels. My heart ached. Tears slipped down my cheeks as I knelt beside his bed and prayed for angels to surround him. That was over ten years ago and not a single night has gone by that I haven't prayed for angels to guard and protect my son.

Psalm 91:11 has become one of my "promise" scriptures. I claim it for myself and other family members as well as Jay. I pray for God to send angels in every situation—at the doctor's office, hospital, home—everywhere. When we travel, I ask God to surround our car or plane with angels—to go before and behind us; to be our guard. In the doctor's office or at the hospital, I pray for barriers of angels to prevent any harm from professionals who may not seek God's wisdom. I pray for angels to surround our home and be visible to anyone who might want to cause destruction or harm.

And though angels never supercede our relationship with Jesus Christ or the voice of the Holy Spirit, I believe our heavenly Father sends these mighty messengers to minister to us in our deepest needs. For that, I am truly thankful.

Lord Jesus, just as angels ministered to You in Your needs, thank You for sending angels to comfort, guard, and minister to us. Thank You for Your unconditional love. Amen.

Louise Tucker Jones is a Gold Medallion Award-winning author and inspirational speaker. She is author of *Dance from the Heart,* co-author of *Extraordinary Kids,* and has published numerous articles.

Re-Gifted

LeAnn Weiss

Trust God from the bottom of your heart; don't try to figure out everything on your own. Listen for God's voice in everything you do, everywhere you go; he's the one who will keep you on track.

Proverbs 3:5-6 THE MESSAGE

For years, I've tucked a little personalized gift in each Encouragement Company order to brighten the recipient's day. I was surprised when one of my bookmarks with personalized scripture dropped out of the envelope from Carole Murphy, one of my new customers.

I skimmed Carole's note, looking for an explanation for the returned bookmark. Carole wrote, "I hope I have not overstepped my bounds in being so honest, but I felt I had to share what was on my heart."

Committing to pray for me, her letter continued, "I am sending this Proverbs 3:5-6 bookmark back to you because it is your verse for today."

I picked up the bookmark and read, "Trust in Me with all of your heart! *Don't* rely on your own limited understanding.

Acknowledge Me in *all* you say and do . . . and I promise I will guide you. Love Always, Your Awesome God. P.S. Remember, I have the advantage of seeing the entire picture and the end product."

My returned bookmark couldn't have been timelier. After days of weighing the pros and cons of a decision, I remained engulfed in indecision. Reading the bookmark, I realized I wasn't practicing the words I'd written. As I prayed, "Father, forgive me for not trusting You with this decision; please show me the way to go," God's peace flooded my heart. I knew I could trust Him with the outcome.

As a single, strong-willed, and independent person, Proverbs 3:5-6 continues to be a life-challenge to me not to rely on my strengths and what I think I should do, but to make sure that I've followed God's superior direction.

Father, forgive me when my independence leads me to leave You out of decisions and areas of my life. When I'm doing my "own thing," remind me to repent and acknowledge You. Thanks that even when I've made mistakes and am tired and confused, You always know the perfect path for me.

LeAnn Weiss began writing paraphrased scriptures in 1992, creating her first personalized book from five years of love letters she had written to God. She became published in 1997 when John Howard invited her to incorporate her paraphrases into the Hugs series.

Bringing It to Pass, Football and All

Patricia Lorenz

Commit thy way unto the Lord; trust also in him; and he shall bring it to pass.

Psalm 37:5 KJV

When the Big Ten University of Wisconsin football team won the right to play in the Hall of Fame Bowl in Tampa in January 1995, I realized that game would be my son Michael's last time to march with the famous UW marching band before he graduated. Although I was a single parent with a small income, I held on to a bigger-than-life dream to see my son march.

In addition, in late November a pilot friend said he could get my younger son, Andrew, and me "*friend passes*" for about $90 each—but we would fly standby. Good news abounded when I remembered we could stay with friends who live near Tampa.

My bubble burst in midair when I read that 30,000 "Wisconsinites" had bought tickets to the Hall of Fame Bowl.

And the airline I'd fly on had only one flight a day to Tampa. What was I thinking? I'd never get on that plane!

A friend suggested I look in the book of Psalms for direction, so I opened my Bible and the first verse I read was Psalm 37:5. Not only did I memorize that verse, but I said it at least a hundred times a day during those weeks before Christmas. The minute I turned the problem over to the Lord, I relaxed completely. And on Christmas Day, Andrew and I were the last two passengers seated on that plane.

Nine days later, after sunning ourselves on Gulf beaches, exploring exotic wonders, and following the Wisconsin marching band as they performed all over Tampa, we watched as the University of Wisconsin defeated the Duke Blue Devils in the Hall of Fame Bowl on a beautiful, sunny, eighty-degree day. Michael's last performance with the band was stellar—but not quite as stellar as my faith in the Lord who brings all things to pass . . . if we just put our trust in Him.

Heavenly Father, thank You for the gift of trust and for easing my stressful life with Your compassionate care and love. Help me to trust You more and worry less so I can live more fully.

Patricia Lorenz is a speaker and author of three books, over 400 articles, and she is a contributor to eleven *Chicken Soup for the Soul* books and dozens of anthologies.

Love Extravagantly

Marita Littauer

Observe how Christ loved us. His love was not cautious but extravagant. He didn't love in order to get something from us but to give everything of himself to us. Love like that.

Ephesians 5:2 THE MESSAGE

My husband Chuck has a large model airplane with a five-foot wingspan. You cannot just tuck it anyplace. In our home it hangs near the peak of the cathedral ceiling in the family room. It is a bright red biplane, sure to be noticed. Since it is important to Chuck, I have accepted it as a conversation piece.

Recently, having spent hours cleaning it, he took it to a model airplane show where it was very popular; and Chuck discovered how valuable it really is. Before he put it back on its hook, he wanted to protect it so he covered it with plastic dry cleaning bags, advertising and all.

Having the airplane hanging there at all is an act of compromise and love. Having it covered with baggy dry cleaning bags with words on them went too far. "I'll never be able to entertain again," I wailed. After my overreaction, I went outside and trimmed my roses. As I took a deep breath, God spoke to me, "Love him extravagantly."

I thought, *Okay. Does it really matter if the airplane has a bag over it? What is more important—that my husband be happy or that I have a lovely home?* "Love extravagantly," I told myself. I came back in and apologized—ready to accept the dry cleaning bags. Meanwhile, he had decided that I was right, and it was really ugly. He took the plane down, removed the dry cleaning bags, and was replacing them with clear plastic wrap that doesn't even show!

But I had learned an important lesson from Ephesians 5:2, and I still love Chuck extravagantly!

Lord, give me strength to love my husband extravagantly in the big things and in the everyday things. Help me make him my priority so he will see Your love through me.

Marita Littauer is a speaker with over twenty years' experience and the author of ten books, including *Personality Puzzle* and *Come As You Are*, and her newest, *Love Extravagantly*.

Engraved On His Hand

Sherrie Eldridge

"Can a mother forget the baby at her breast and have no compassion on the child she has borne? Though she may forget, I will not forget you! See, I have engraved you on the palms of my hands; your walls are ever before me."

Isaiah 49:15-16 NIV

At forty-seven years of age, after years of fruitless searching for my birth mother, I found her within days of hiring an adoption professional. The first time I met my birth mother, we met by phone. We talked into the wee hours of the night, and as I later lay sleepless in bed, feelings of completeness overwhelmed me.

Within two weeks, at her request, my husband and I were on a plane bound for her home. My birth mother and I were to be reunited.

At the suggestion of the adoption professional, I gave her a photograph album of my life from birth until the present. I fantasized that we would sit on the couch, as mother and daughter, and she'd tell me how proud she was of me as I retold my history.

Much to my dismay, she flipped through the pages, shoved the book aside, saying, "You sure were cute." From that time forward, things began to sour.

Two days after returning home I called to thank her. The moment I heard the tone of her voice, I had a sick feeling in my stomach. She abusively turned everything about me to the most negative interpretation possible and announced her desire for no further contact.

I could hear her caustic words with my ears, but in my spirit I heard the words of Isaiah 49:15. I knew that Jesus was standing with me in that moment when my deepest fear was becoming a reality. I ran to my husband and fell into his arms, sobbing and numb.

Looking back, I realize that without this experience I wouldn't know that God's love and comfort are far deeper than any rejection life can throw at you.

Lord, thank You that Your love and comfort are so much deeper than any human rejection. I thought I was searching for my birth mother's arms, but I was really searching for Yours.

Sherrie Eldridge is an internationally known speaker on the subject of adoption, the author of *Twenty Things Adopted Kids Wish Their Adoptive Parents Knew,* and the President of Jewel Among Jewels Adoption Network, Inc.

Free to Go

Sharon Jaynes

"You will know the truth, and the truth will set you free."
John 8:32 NIV

Many colorful characters lived in Andy Griffith's fictitious town of Mayberry, one of which was Otis, the town drunk. Many times, Otis was arrested for public drunkenness and placed in jail until he sobered up. After a good night's sleep and a hearty breakfast prepared by Aunt Bea, the ever-repentant Otis was free to go. If he was ready to leave incarceration before the law enforcement officers arrived for work, Otis simply stuck his hand through the jail cell bars, reached for the key hanging on the wall outside his door, and let himself go free. On a few occasions, Otis stumbled into the jailhouse unescorted, locked himself in the cell, and placed the key back on the nail on the wall.

This was always a comical scene, but it reminds me of the jail we lock ourselves into when we believe the lies of Satan.

John 10:10 states that the thief comes only to kill, steal, and destroy. His weapon of choice is lies. He whispers: *Nobody loves you, God could never forgive you, you are a bad mother, wife, Christian, etc.* Of course these are lies that he uses to hold us in the chains of inferiority, insecurity, and inadequacy.

John 8:32 holds the key to freedom. "*You will know the truth, and the truth will set you free.*" Understanding that you are an adopted child, forgiven in Christ, sets you free from the bondage of inferiority. Understanding the gifts you have in Christ—His Holy Spirit within you, spiritual abilities to make you a valued member of His family, and a new life—sets you free from the bondage of inadequacy. Understanding that you are in Christ and seated right now at God's right hand with Him on His throne sets you free from the bondage of insecurity.

The key to freedom is within our reach—right in God's Word. Will you be free?

Dear Lord, help me reach through the prison doors and grasp the key to freedom hanging on the nail— the nail on the Cross of Calvary.

Sharon Jaynes is the author of *Being a Great Mom—Raising Great Kids* and *Ultimate Makeover*, a radio co-host for Proverbs 31 Ministries, and a popular conference speaker from coast to coast.

Let Go

Lynn D. Morrissey

He is like a tree planted by streams of water, which yields its fruit in season and whose leaf does not wither. Whatever he does prospers.

Psalm 1:3 NIV

Leave my twenty-year career, Lord? Stay home with a baby everyday without any adult company? When I was forty, I wrestled with God over the "surprise" birth of my daughter Sheridan. Father, I'll sink into depression. How can I cope without people and work? They keep me going!

Patiently, the Lord pried loose my grip. As I walked in autumn woods, God guided my decision through the example of colorful leaves, clinging tenaciously to branches, struggling to hold on. Then, as if by some knowledge of God's command, with each gust of wind, they simply let go, entering a graceful waltz, pirouetting with abandon in the breeze. Beauty and freedom characterized their release. I "heard" God's inaudible command, "Lynn, let go!" I gave my employer notice, committing to enter whatever dance God was choreographing.

Times of depression and loneliness ensued. I was a "winter tree," stripped of the lush foliage of professional purpose, accolades, and friendships. Yet I knew that though the tree looked dead, it lived; its life wasn't in its leaves, but in its roots. Psalm 1:3 became my lifeline, ensuring me that as I rooted myself in God I'd bear future fruit.

Trees don't sin by complaining. They bloom in season; and in times of barrenness, their leafless limbs raise in praise to their Maker. Stripped of foliage, they have an unparalleled opportunity to behold stars shining like jewels between their branches.

I decided to behold life's "stars" I'd been too blindsided to see—brilliant constellations of blessings, lighting my darkness—more time with my daughter and for my dream of writing and speaking.

When, like the autumn leaf, I let go, I entered the beauty of God's dance—finally free to follow Him fully—experiencing the knowledge that the only gulf into which I could fall was the palm of my Partner's hand.

Lord, help me to remember that times of barrenness are never permanent. As I root myself in You, imbibing the living waters of Your Word, I will always succeed.

Lynn D. Morrissey is editor of *Seasons of a Woman's Heart* and *Treasures of a Woman's Heart*, contributing author to numerous best-sellers, and CLASS speaker specializing in journaling and women's topics.

Everlasting Arms

Linda Evans Shepherd

The eternal God is your refuge, and
underneath are the everlasting arms.
Deuteronomy 33:27 NIV

I knew I was on borrowed time. It was 9 P.M. and my then three-year-old son, Jimmy, was exhausted after an evening of shopping at the mall.

I checked my watch. *How had it gotten so late?* Holding Jimmy's small hand in mine, I led him toward the parking lot exit of a department store. Suddenly, Jimmy fell at my feet, hugging one of my snow boots for all that it was worth.

"Mom, I'm too tired to go on. Could you just drag me for a while?"

I tried not to chuckle as I imagined pulling my child through the store by my leg.

Leaning down, I looked into his sleepy, blue eyes. "No, honey, but I can carry you."

I scooped him into my arms and cradled my exhausted child to my heart. As I snapped him into his car seat, I wondered, *How many times have I thrown myself at God's feet and said, "God, could You just drag me for a while?"*

But God doesn't want to drag me through the muck. He prefers to scoop me into His arms and carry me.

This picture of God cradling me next to His heart reminds me of one of my favorite scriptures: "*The eternal God is your refuge, and underneath are the everlasting arms.*"

Those everlasting arms have carried me through the heartache of a violent car accident that paralyzed my infant daughter; they've carried me to the other side of the valley of the shadow of death; they've carried me when I was too exhausted to go on.

What a joy to know that no matter what obstacle blocks my way, I can trust God to carry me on the journey He has set before me.

Dear Lord, I love the idea that Your arms surround me.
Thank You for refusing to rake me through the muck
but for carrying me through my most difficult days.

Linda Evans Shepherd is the host of Right to the Heart Radio, a one-minute feature aired throughout the country, and the founder of Advanced Writers & Speakers Association.

A Wimp in Good Company!

Robi Lipscomb

After the earthquake came a fire, but the Lord was not in the fire. And after the fire came a gentle whisper.

1 Kings 19:12 NIV

"God, speak to me!"

"What are you doing here, Elijah?" (1 Kings 19:9).

Elijah cried out for God to end his life in the desert. I have prayed that prayer. *Lord, take me now, I cannot go on!*

Elijah performed amazing things! But, when Queen Jezebel threatened to kill him, he ran to the desert. He found a tree, laid down, and prayed, "I have had enough, Lord. Take my life."

Usually our prayer to die comes after our greatest spiritual victory, when we are burned out. Fortunately, God doesn't always give us what we ask for! God says, "What are you doing here?"

As if God didn't already know.

God knew the answer to the question He posed to Elijah, and He knows the answer when He poses it to me. Elijah responded to God with childlike behavior. I say to God, "Can't I just go to heaven and be done?" Elijah and I are much alike.

Instead of a parental lecture to Elijah, God simply told Elijah to go stand on the mountain He was about to pass by! Elijah obeyed. The mountains were torn apart by a great wind; there was an earthquake and fire. But God was not in those. Next was a gentle whisper, and God was in the whisper. God's will and power were in the wind, earthquake, and fire, but God spoke to Elijah in a whisper.

And He speaks to me in a whisper as well when I quiet down, turn back to Him in prayer, and read His Word. My heart is re-broken for those to whom God has called me to minister and, like Elijah, I am ready to go out and live again.

In a whisper God draws near when we are too tired to go on. We want God to come to us loud and clear. But the most personal voice of God is a whisper.

God, let me be still and know You are God. Come close and whisper to me. Thank You that You are always, even in my darkest moments, as close as a whisper.

Author, speaker, wife, and mother of two teenage boys, Robi Lipscomb shares God with as much energy and joy as the youth with whom she interacts!

Eyes Upon God

Christin Ditchfield

We have no power to face this vast army that is attacking us.
We do not know what to do, but our eyes are upon you.

2 Chronicles 20:12 NIV

King Jehoshaphat and his tiny nation found themselves in dire circumstances—their enemies had gathered a vast army against them and were soon approaching. The king called the people of Judah to fast and pray. Young and old, men, women, and children—all gathered at the temple to stand before the Lord.

Jehoshaphat cried out to God, reminding Him of His promise to care for them. He declared the nation's commitment to wait on God for deliverance, and he referred specifically to the crisis at hand—the imminent attack of the enemy. The king concluded his prayer simply: "*We do not know what to do, but our eyes are upon you.*"

So many times I've found myself completely overwhelmed by the circumstances of life. In my prayers for my loved ones, myself, or our nation, I've cried out to God with the words of King Jehoshaphat: "*We do not know what to do, but our eyes are upon you.*" It's quickly become one of my favorite Bible prayers.

The Scripture says that those who look to the Lord will never be ashamed. They will not be forsaken. As Jehoshaphat and his people waited on God, they received this precious promise from Him: "*Do not be afraid or discouraged because of this vast army. For the battle is not yours, but God's. . . . Stand firm and see the deliverance the Lord will give you*" (2 Chronicles 20:15,17).

God offers that same assurance to you and me today.

Lord, I thank You that when I am weak, You are strong.
You are my shield, my fortress, and my defense.
Help me to keep my eyes fixed upon You.

Christin Ditchfield is an author, conference speaker, and host of the nationally syndicated radio program, *Take It to Heart!*

Prescription for Insomnia

Pamela Stephens

I lie down and sleep; I wake again,
because the Lord sustains me.
Psalm 3:5 NIV

I have suffered many fearful, sleepless nights in my past. I remember when I lay awake at night thinking about the next morning's outpatient surgery, running many different scenarios through my head. Would the lab results come back cancerous or benign? Having lost my mother to breast cancer, the seed of unease is ever ready to bloom forth with fear and loathing.

On other occasions, there were the nights when a child was away from home because of poor choices. I didn't know where she was laying her head, but I knew that as parents we were doing the "right" thing. Still, wondering about my child's safety, it felt terribly "wrong" by cover of night. I remember praying, "God, You alone know where she is tonight and whom she is with. Guide her back safely to YOU first and then to us. Help my unbelief, because I don't know how all of this will turn out. Help us all to REST safely in You, Lord." I finally slept, knowing the Lord was watching over my child, no matter where she was.

My Lord watches over me when the enemies of fear, worry, frustration, doubt, and anger surround me on every side. He slaps each one of those enemies in the face, insulting them for accosting me, and removes the hold of panic on my heart. He replaces the enemies' harassment with peace and safety for His name's sake and allows my mind to rest in His keeping. Psalm 3:5 has taught me these truths and given me the ability to rest in the midst of turmoil because He really does sustain me.

Thank You, Lord, that we can come to You and expect Your peace, if we have given our hearts to You. Help us to remember to turn to You immediately when situations arise, so we can lie down and sleep at night.

Pamela Stephens is married with two grown daughters and two grandsons. She loves to speak for women's retreats and other events and shares how God has taught her many valuable lessons through her life's experiences.

Rescue Me

Karen Porter

He reached down from on high and took hold of me;
he drew me out of deep waters.
Psalm 18:16 NIV

Behind our house near the fence is a beautiful stand of lilies. They are blooming in red, yellow, purple, and orange. I don't know how they survived. Years ago, we dug them up at Grandmother's house to bring them to our home but forgot to plant them for much too long. We finally put them in the flowerbed and they miraculously lived. Later the cows leaned over the fence and chewed them to the ground. Just when they sprang up again, Dad mowed them flat. We've forgotten to water or feed them and now weeds surround them. But there they are—brightly blooming and beautiful. It is as if God reached down and pulled them up to stand straight and glorious.

When my busy, breakneck schedule overwhelms me, I feel as though I've been chewed down to the nub. Sometimes hurtful or careless words mow me down. Most often my defeats are because I've blown it by allowing anger, impatience, or unforgiveness to rule my day. The weeds creep in because I've failed to regularly get food and water from God's Word. But even when I am in deep weeds, He reaches down and pulls me up. No matter how far my trouble takes me, I am never out of His reach.

He sees my potential instead of my failures. He reaches down, brings me up, and helps me blossom. When He takes me in His hand, I flourish and thrive.

Psalm 18:16 reminds me that no matter how much trouble I get into, my God of the second chance is ready to rescue me. Sometimes when I evaluate my life, all I see are my failures and mistakes—then I remember Grandmother's lilies.

Lord, when things seem out of control and I've been cut down, please help me see Your strong and sure hands reaching for me.

Karen Porter is an author and speaker from Texas where she is also vice president of a major food company. She is co-author of *Bible Seeds*.

Words

Naomi Rhode

Let the words of my mouth and the meditation of my heart be acceptable in Your sight, O LORD, my rock and my Redeemer.

Psalm 19:14 NASB

Are you fascinated with words? Are you intrigued by their power to support, to praise, and encourage; to attack, wound, tear down, or tarnish? I am. Raised by parents who were educators in both public and Christian sectors, as well as pastor and speakers, words became a profound part of my life. Often, my father would speak of "the value of little things," using the well-read nursery rhyme:

For want of a nail, the shoe was lost
For want of a shoe, the horse was lost
For want of a horse, the battle was lost
For want of the battle, the nation was lost
All for the want of a horseshoe nail.

And then he would speak of pursuing the mastery of words, the ability to use them to encourage, build bridges between people, and ultimately and even foremost, to share the Word, (God's words spoken in the Bible) with a needy people.

I'm fascinated that Amos prophesies a "famine of words" because of the sins of the people, which led to a 400-year period of *no words* from God, broken by *The Word*, a title applied to the Son of God. Jesus ultimately left us with the Word of God and himself, *The Word*, who dwells within us as believers.

Thus, as a professional speaker and writer, I pray my favorite scripture before I speak: *"Let the words of my mouth* [how very important and well chosen they must be] *and the meditation of my heart* [which always precede my words] *be acceptable in Your sight* [which is all that really matters], *O LORD, my rock and my Redeemer."*

This can happen only as I reflect on the power and truth of *His* words.

Father, thank You for Your vast and rich legacy of words.
Thank You for sending Your Son, The Word, to
dwell richly in our hearts. Empower us with Your
vocabulary, rich and right for every need. Amen.

Naomi Rhode, CSP, CPAE Speaker Hall of Fame, Past President National Speakers Association, author of *The Gift of Family: A Legacy of Love*, and *More Beautiful than Diamonds: The Gift of Friendship*.

Friendship with God

Vickey Banks

Friendship with God is reserved for those who reverence him. With them alone he shares the secrets of his promises.

Psalm 25:14 TLB

"You should read your Bible every day," the preacher at my friend's church camp emphatically said. I wanted to do what was right. The only problem was I had never seen anyone *other* than a preacher read the Bible, and I had no idea how to approach it! Too fearful that I would be embarrassed by sounding as spiritually inferior as I was sure I was, I didn't dare ask anyone for help.

Confident I would never understand the Old Testament on my own, I turned to the book of Matthew and began to read a few verses every night before I went to bed. I liked the stories, but I didn't see how they related to me personally. After four years of reading the Bible and rolling over to go to sleep, I realized there was more to it than my first impressions and I longed to understand more of what I read.

When I went to college, I finally learned through a non-denominational campus ministry how to purposely read the Bible and ask myself questions that would help me apply it to my everyday life. No longer was reading the Bible just something I was supposed to do. Suddenly, God and His Word got incredibly personal to me! I realized that by putting His love for me on paper, God enabled me to hold His very words in my hands and to actually *read* His secrets—secrets He was eager to share with me!

Once I began to read and respond to God's Word with the reverence it deserved, I experienced something I thought was far beyond my reach: friendship with God.

So, open up your Bible today and listen closely. God has secrets to share and He is looking for a friend with whom to share them. Are you listening?

God, You truly are my most faithful friend.
Thank You again and again for sharing Your
secrets with me. Help me to be a better listener.

Vickey Banks loves to encourage and equip others to experience deeper intimacy with God. Psalm 25:14 was the inspiration for her book, *Sharing His Secrets: Intimate Insights from the Women Who Knew Jesus.*

There Is One Thing I Want

Cindi McMenamin

One thing I ask of the Lord, *this is what I seek: that I may dwell in the house of the* Lord *all the days of my life, to gaze upon the beauty of the* Lord *and to seek him in his temple.*

Psalm 27:4 NIV

Have you ever asked the Lord to change your husband? I did. "Please change his heart, Lord," I would pray. "Give him the ability to express himself to me in a way that fills my heart's hunger."

But God wanted to change my heart instead, and He wanted to be the One to satisfy the hunger. "Seek Me like my servant David did," God seemed to be saying to me through His Word. "Only I can fill your heart's hunger."

I realized that if David—who was described as "a man after God's own heart"—wanted only one thing and that one thing was intimacy with God, I too had to learn how to say, "There is *one thing* I want . . . and it's You, O God."

So I began to look to the Lord to be my Husband. I began to seek His face through worship and study of His Word. And I began to pray for a heart to want Him more than anything else. As I did that, He faithfully showed me that when I seek Him first, all those other things follow like wrappings on the prize.

I must admit, there are still days when I want something other than Him—more harmony in my marriage, a child who gladly obeys, a bigger and more effective ministry, or a life in which finances are never a concern. Although some of those things I want are truly good . . . they are not enough. They have never, in and of themselves, satisfied. And they never will. Jesus must always be the *one thing* I want or I will always long for something more.

When He becomes *all* I want, perhaps then I will be on my way to becoming all He wants as well.

O LORD, may I become so consumed with a desire
for You that the rest of this world loses its appeal.
Give me a heart like David so I will want to seek Your face.

Cindi McMenamin is a pastor's wife, mother, national conference speaker, and author of the books *Heart Hunger* and *When Women Walk Alone*.

All the Way Home

M. L. Chandler

I will instruct you (says the Lord) and guide
you along the best pathway for your life;
I will advise you and watch your progress.
Psalm 32:8 TLB

My subject for a women's church retreat, *Count It All Joy,* needed swift revisions when, on arrival at a conference site, I learned that the pastor's college-age daughter had been murdered about a month ago. No one had told me!

Only my all-knowing Friend, Jesus, could instruct me as I listened, learned details, and sought the direction of the Holy Spirit. I e-mailed my support team and telephoned my husband for intercession. Covered by prayer, weekend participants began a God-guided journey with me through the Word to discover His ultimate joy.

How easy it is to unintentionally "goof up" when facing a new audience. Simple mistakes happen—like too much eye shadow, dangling earrings, or a pants suit when others are in floor-length dresses. Every day is an adventure! Knowing that Jesus instructs and guides gives me daily courage and comfort. But sometimes more serious issues lie concealed.

Another time, I heard on arrival at a banquet site: "Your invitation to speak has been canceled." *Why? What happened? I've driven several hours in the rain; what could have gone wrong?* The program chairperson told me that their pastor had heard that I'd been divorced—decades ago. The youth band would perform that evening, replacing me.

On the spot I had to decide whether to attempt to change the mind of one in authority or to retreat. "*Help me. I need guidance, Lord!*" I prayed. Understanding the group would not be receptive to any message not blessed by their pastor, I graciously accepted their wishes.

Whether a seemingly small stumbling block or an issue that looms large, I know when God guides my way it will be the best pathway—all the way home.

Thank You, Jesus, for instructing me. Every day I need a caring Friend, and You are there. Wherever, whenever, I can trust Your direction. You even keep me from getting into trouble!

Marjorie Lee "ML" Chandler writes and speaks to bring hope to those who hurt, especially in family relationships. Her book, *After Your Child Divorces*, encourages parents of adult children to re-bond their family circle.

The Weight of Broken Promises

Jill Rigby

I sought the Lord, and he answered me; he delivered me from all my fears. Those who look to him are radiant; their faces are never covered with shame.

Psalm 34:4-5 NIV

When I looked in the mirror I couldn't find myself. The weight of broken promises left my face barren, lifeless; my eyes were empty, void of passion. I had fallen so low that I was unable to reach up to the only One who could truly help me. Mother had taken the boys to school because I couldn't find the courage to face the world. A broken heart sent me so deep into despair that I was paralyzed with fear. I was afraid to be alone, terrified of the future.

I was so exhausted I could barely speak, but I was finally ready to talk to Him. As I felt the warmth of the sun on my face, I felt His presence in the midst of my sorrow for the first time in weeks. Very slowly, I lifted my head toward heaven; and with all the breath I could find, I whispered to the Lord, "I don't know what You're going to do with my ruined life, but it's Yours. It's *all* Yours." The sun gleamed through the kitchen window as I stood waiting for an answer. As I turned to leave the kitchen, I looked back and said, "I can't help You with my life; I can't even help myself."

In the midst of ceasing to live, I learned the secret to living—total abandonment. I couldn't live until I gave *all* of myself to the Lord. When I quietly turned to Him, I found the courage to face the world again. Most glorious of all, I was delivered from the shame of failure that had broken me.

O Lord, thank You for answering my cry for deliverance. May my face radiate Your healing grace and may my heart extend Your love to others in need of Your touch. Amen.

Jill Rigby carries a message of hope to women through her seminar, *Yes, Sir, Yes, Sir! The Joy of Obedience*. She is the author of *Manners of the Heart* and *Manners of the Heart at Home*.

The Desires of His Heart

Eva Marie Everson

Delight thyself also in the LORD; and he shall give thee the desires of thine heart.

Psalm 37:4 KJV

I'd always wanted to be a writer. Even as a young child, I can remember the desire to put pen to paper. But at twelve, when asked what I wanted to be "when I grew up," and I answered, "A writer," my reply was met by chuckles and discouragement. So I became a nurse instead.

Years went by, children grew up, and I began to take daily walks filled with heavenly chats. "Lord," I'd begin. "You know the desire of my heart. The desire of my heart is to serve You by speaking and writing." Nearly every day, I said that same prayer. But no doors opened for me. Then, one day as I took my walk, I said, "Lord, You know the desire of my heart. The desire of my heart is to serve You by speaking and writing."

Suddenly I stopped. "No," I said. "The desire of my heart is *not* to serve You with my speaking and writing. The desire of my heart is to serve You. Period. And if I have to lay that baby on the altar, I will."

The floodgates opened. In a short period of time, I signed publishing contracts and began to speak all over the country. At various conferences I'm sometimes asked how God did so much in so little time. I smile. This isn't about the books, the speaking topics, the teaching material—and it certainly isn't about me! It wasn't until God showed me the misguided direction of my will and I delighted in Him alone that my ministry was truly born. This is about Him. It's all about Him and the story of what happens when we align our will to His will. Only then will the desires of our heart be met . . . *and beyond!*

Lord, help me to know that my walk is about delighting in You . . . not about the desires of my heart. Help me to place my will within Your will. I will praise Your name forever.

Eva Marie Everson's work includes *Summon the Shadows*, *Shadow of Dreams*, *True Love*, and *One True Vow*. She is a nationally recognized speaker and Bible teacher.

He Is Listening

Teresa Griggs

Find rest, O my soul, in God alone; my hope comes from him. He alone is my rock and my salvation; he is my fortress, I will not be shaken. My salvation and my honor depend on God; he is my mighty rock, my refuge. Trust in him at all times, O people; pour out your hearts to him, for God is our refuge.

Psalm 62:5-8 NIV

When my oldest son, Chris, was in the sixth grade, we moved from Denver to Sikeston, Missouri. At a difficult age, Chris didn't have an easy time fitting into life at Sikeston. He felt the kids at school didn't like him. It became such a problem that we went to a Christian counselor. She helped me see that when Chris told me how others treated him, he didn't need me to fix it, which is exactly what I tried to do. She explained, "All he really needs is for you to listen. Affirm to him that you are giving him your full attention by repeating back to him what he just told you." Simply sharing the pain with him was enough.

I have found in my life that God's listening ear when I share my pain is exactly what I need from Him. I know He is not going to always fix the situation. My nine-year-old daughter, Mallory, died of a rare blood disorder on November 22, 1995. That situation is not going to change, but I need to pour out my feelings and pain to God anyway. I know that He is listening. He gives me affirmation. Each time I go to Him, He takes me in His Word to passages of comfort and peace. As Psalm 62 tells me, I can find rest in God alone as I pour out my heart to Him. So I do. He is my hope, my strength. I trust in Him at all times for He is my refuge! And He is yours too. He knows, He cares, He is listening!

Dear Lord, thank You for listening. I am so grateful that I can find rest in You alone as I pour out my heart to You. You are my hope, my strength. I trust You at all times because You are my refuge. Amen.

Teresa Griggs reaches others through her compassionate speaking, writing, and singing ministry. She is a wife, mother, and grandmother seeking to share God's goodness and the gospel message of Jesus Christ our Lord.

Those Who Honor God

Pam Farrell

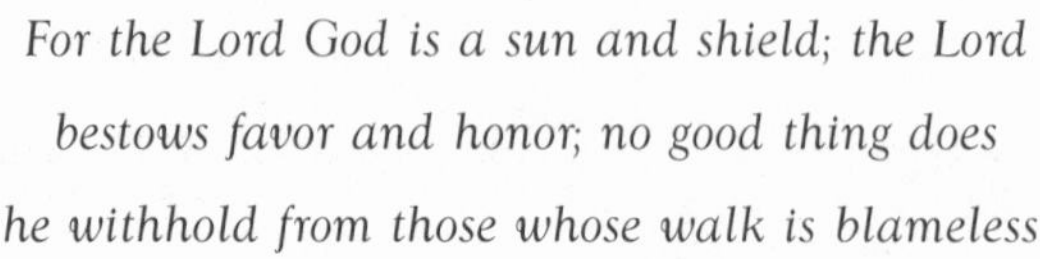

For the Lord God is a sun and shield; the Lord bestows favor and honor; no good thing does he withhold from those whose walk is blameless.

Psalm 84:11 NIV

As a college student, when I read that Psalm, the principle seemed clear: *Those who honor God, God honors*.

Shortly after, I read how I should not be unequally yoked with an unbeliever; so I broke up with a boyfriend. After that I met Bill. Then I read how God wanted my heart to be pure, so Bill and I ran our relationship so that all our choices would be above reproach—we decided not to kiss until we were engaged, and we dated so that our hearts could remain pure before God moment by moment. Now I see the fruit of that choice: a marriage that defies all odds, both of us from dysfunctional homes—married at twenty, yet Bill and I lead marriage conferences and have a happy, twenty-year marriage!

Later, as a first-time mother, I cried out to God, "Parent me, so I can parent Brock." Then God, through His Word, laid out parenting priorities. At eighteen, Brock, the founder of Fellowship of Christian Athletes on his campus, a 4.0 student, and a three-sport athlete, was honored with a commendation from our state governor for San Diego Citizen Athlete. The NFL retired players gave him a sizable scholarship and the National Football Hall of Fame Foundation honored him with the Scholar, Leader, Athlete Award.

I know because of Psalm 84:11 that God is the One who has bestowed upon me favor and honor as I have made it my business, with the strength He supplies, to honor His wishes.

Lord, by faith I took You at Your Word and am thrilled with the result. I don't know how, and I don't know when, but those who honor God, God honors. Honor the readers of this book as they honor Your Word. Amen.

Pam Farrell is an international speaker and author of more than fourteen books, including best-selling *Men Are Like Waffles, Women Are Like Spaghetti*, *Woman of Influence*, and *The Treasure Inside Your Child.*

Secret Place

Sharon Hoffman

He who dwells in the secret place of the Most High
shall abide under the shadow of the Almighty.

Psalm 91:1 NKJV

Every little girl needs a private, secret place where she can be settled and secure, as does every woman. We need a place where we can run when we are in great need or when we feel we just cannot take it anymore.

When I was a child we lived in a large, roomy parsonage right next door to the church. Between the buildings was a narrow corridor with a small porch and steps leading up to a "secret" side entrance into the church. Even now I can picture myself sitting on those steps. I would go there when I was afraid, in trouble, or occasionally needed to be alone just to ponder.

It was my very own secret hiding place. I felt complete safety and peace there. Free to be *me!*

The psalmist says that the one who dwells in the secret place finds peace and comfort. The true secret place is the place where we spend time praying and seeking God—abiding and taking up permanent residence there. It's where we trust God and completely rely on Him. In that place we abide under the protective shadow of His wings. He wants us to run to Him! Just imagine. Instead of worrying, in our secret place we can rest in His care.

Some people run to alcohol as their hiding place. Others use television or drugs. Some just hide and pull covers up over their heads. However, instead of looking to what the world offers, God longs for us to find our hiding place in Him. God wants us to take refuge in the "secret place" under the protective shadow of His wings. He wants us to run to Him!

Father God, I run right now to my secret hiding place . . . into Your presence. I commit myself entirely unto You. I cast all my cares on You because I know that You care for me. I thank You, my God, that I am in You and You are in me. In my secret place under the shadow of Your wings, my heart need not be troubled or afraid.

Sharon Hoffman impacts women's lives around the world as a speaker, author of five books, and the founder of GIFTed Women—Godly Influencers for Today. She and her husband, who is a pastor, live in North Carolina.

The Father's Life-Giving Plan

Lee Ezell

For you created my inmost being; you knit me together in my mother's womb. . . . My frame was not hidden from you when I was made in the secret place . . . your eyes saw my unformed body.

Psalm 139:13,15-16 NIV

Discovering I was pregnant put me over the edge. I was an "unwanted child" now pregnant with an unwanted child. Boy! Was I thrilled that dark night when I found Psalm 139:13,15-16! As a brand-new Christian I wasn't sure this promise counted for *me*. I was in a desperate state; so as I read these verses, they shocked me. If *they* were true, then my alcoholic father was wrong—I *wasn't* a mistake. Apparently, even though a couple decides when to make love, God decides when to make life. These verses comforted me because as a virgin teenager and a brand-new Christian, I had been raped. And now another life had begun.

I drifted until I found my moorings through these verses. They convinced me that abortion is too permanent an answer for a temporary problem. I would give birth to that baby girl and have her adopted in the State of California Adoptions network. She became the "missing piece" of my life.

Only God could have coordinated the ringing of my phone years later when a female voice said, "Hello, you've never met me, but you are my mother." And in that first conversation this daughter, Julie, let me know I was a grandmother and tried to lead me to Jesus on the phone! Our reunion has been chronicled in my book, *The Missing Piece*, and led us through a groundswell of media appearances on all the secular TV and radio talk shows. What a thrill to hear this girl quote these beautiful Bible verses and remark, "I'm so glad I did not get the death penalty for the crime of my father!" How wonderful that God let her know that her life was a part of His plan through the same scripture He's used to teach me!

Father God, thanks for Your plan for life. We acknowledge You were the One who decided to give us life, and in sending Your Son to die for us, You provided eternal life. We are grateful! Amen.

Lee Ezell is a popular speaker and author of eight books. Lee lives in Southern California and divides her time between writing and her full-time speaking schedule.

Wholehearted Trust

Kathe Wunnenberg

Trust in the Lord with all of your heart
and lean not on your own understanding.
Proverbs 3:5 NIV

"Will you marry me?"

I'll never forget the day my college sweetheart knelt on one knee, gazed lovingly into my eyes, and asked me that question. After what seemed to be an eternity of silence, I finally blurted out, *"I'm 95 percent sure!"*

Wholehearted commitment has always been difficult for me because it requires me to trust someone else. Perhaps I feel this way because I have experienced dashed dreams and broken trust throughout my life: my parents' divorce, a friend's betrayal, a church division, family member's substance abuse, and my own infertility. People and circumstances I thought I could depend on seemed to always fall short and break my heart. So I began to guard it. In a sense I compartmentalized my heart. Outwardly I appeared enthusiastic and willing to risk in relationships and circumstances, but inwardly I knew that my secret heart compartment defended my control over my life and my true self.

Although I loved God and knew Him personally, the civil war within my heart raged until I discovered in the fourteenth week of my "miracle pregnancy" that my child had a fatal birth defect. Over the next twenty-six weeks of my pregnancy I clung to the truth of Proverbs 3:5. God used it to transform my guarded heart into a trusting heart. Although I didn't know what the future held, I rested in the certainty of who held the future. Although my heart was broken yet another time when my son was ushered into heaven, I knew God loved me and He understood the pain of losing a son. I chose to trust Him with all of my questions, anger, and sorrow as I journeyed through grief. He was faithful to meet me where I was, and He still does.

Lord, transform my guarded heart into a trusting heart. Help me to trust You with all of my heart. Today I release control of my life to You. Thank You for being trustworthy and for loving me wholeheartedly. Amen.

Kathe Wunnenberg is a speaker and the author of *Grieving the Child I Never Knew* and *Grieving the Loss of a Loved One*. She married her college sweetheart; they live in Phoenix with their three sons.

The Daisy Dance

Alice Gray

His banner over me is love.

Song of Solomon 2:4 NIV

Brennan Manning tells a touching story about a priest walking along a country road near his parish. He noticed an old peasant kneeling at the side of the road praying. The priest walked over and gently placed his hand on the old man's shoulder and said, "You must be very close to the Lord." The peasant paused for a moment and then looked up at the priest with clear blue eyes. A broad smile deepened the wrinkles in his tanned face as he replied, "Yes, the Lord is very fond of me."[1]

What a wonderful thought! The Lord is very fond of me. He is very fond of you. His banner over us isn't judgment or criticism or disapproval. His banner over us is love!

When I was in the third grade, I had a tremendous crush on a boy named Richard. At recess, Richard pulled the ribbons on my blond braids and I imagined that he cared about me too. Like two detectives searching for proof, my best friend Maggie and I picked a daisy and then huddled in the fresh mowed grass carefully pulling off the delicate white petals, "He loves me . . . he loves me not. He loves me . . . he loves me not," wondering how the daisy game would end.

It is so different with the Lord. I never have to wonder. "He loves me. He loves me. He loves me. He loves me." Just thinking about it makes my heart dance.

Dear Lord, there are so many times when I am outside the popularity circle. Like a girl at the dance without a partner. Maybe I've disappointed someone or I just can't measure up even when I try. But You open Your arms and remind me that I am always inside the circle of Your love. Thank You for holding me close.

Alice Gray is an ordinary woman loved by an extraordinary God. She is the creator and compiler of the best-selling *Stories for the Heart*™ books.

[1]Brennan Manning, *Abba's Child: The Cry of the Heart for Intimate Belonging* (Colorado Springs: NavPress, 1994), 64.

Here I Am! Send Me!

Nancy Moser

Then I heard the voice of the Lord saying, "Whom shall I send? And who will go for us?" And I said, "Here am I. Send me!"

Isaiah 6:8 NIV

Prior to 1995 I had set out to be a famous (and hopefully rich!) author. Toward that end I wrote five secular novels—and got rejected repeatedly. I had been a casual Christian for forty of my forty-seven years. I didn't go to church except on Easter Sunday and only prayed when I needed something. But eventually, one of those rejections got my attention. And God's little voice niggled at me (just like in the Isaiah verse) continually. I turned away from the secular market and toward Him—even though I didn't know Him. Then on March 14, 1995, I finally listened to God's voice—and answered. On that day, I dedicated all my writing to this persistent Person who wouldn't leave me alone.

With the act of saying, "Here am I! Send me!" my entire life changed. I put aside my secular novels (after a pathetic attempt to paste God in) and started fresh. With Him in mind, I wrote my first Christian novel in two months (a feat not duplicated). Since then I've had seven books published, with six more on the way. Is this because I'm such a great writer? Alas, no. It's because I'm finally on the road God wants me to walk.

That's the challenge for all of us. To say yes to God *before* we know the details. To blatantly, boldly open ourselves up to Him and say, "Yes, Lord! Do it! Whatever *You* want."

I have a motto I try to live by: God's way or no way. Which leads me to my second favorite verse, Isaiah 30:21 NIV: *"Whether you turn to the right or to the left, your ears will hear a voice behind you, saying, 'This is the way; walk in it.'"*

Oh, yes . . . say yes to *His* way!

Lord, I want to say yes to You, but I'm afraid.
What will You want from me? Can I do it?
Help me to trust You. Help me surrender and say, "Yes!"

Nancy Moser is the author of six novels with a common theme of finding our unique purpose and saying "yes!" to God. They include *The Mustard Seed* series, *The Seat Beside Me*, and *Time Lottery*.

Stayed On Thee

Fran Caffey Sandin

You will keep in perfect peace him whose
mind is steadfast, because he trusts in you.
Isaiah 26:3 NIV

Our seventeen-month-old son Jeffrey became feverish one Sunday in 1974. A trip to the emergency room resulted in admittance with a diagnosis of bacterial meningitis. On Monday morning he was transferred to Children's Medical Center in Dallas. Despite all the proper medications and state-of-the-art treatment, the ravages of the illness prevailed.

Just prior, I had memorized and meditated upon Isaiah 26:3. As the busy wife of a physician and mother of three preschoolers, I depended upon daily devotions for inspiration, but I could never have imagined the degree to which I would need His perfect peace in only a matter of hours.

By Thursday afternoon, the doctors requested a conference. Jeffrey's mechanical support system was no longer sustaining life but prolonging death; the time had come to say good-bye to our precious little boy. As my husband and I walked hand in hand through the ICU doorway, I could feel the Lord hugging me, enfolding me with His grace and love. "I have peace," I whispered through my tears, knowing it had to be a supernatural peace. In a soul-wrenching moment of releasing our son, I knew that because of my Savior, Jesus Christ, I would see Jeffrey again in Heaven.

Through the years as other painful and difficult circumstances have arisen, I continue to gain courage and strength from this verse. Sometimes I become anxious until I remember that God is always greater. When my mind is glued upon Him, His character and His heart, life becomes easier. Whatever we trust to the world will be limited to time and space, but whatever we entrust to God will last for eternity.

Dear Father, thank You that You are the Rock of Ages and You never change. Thank You that when we trust You, You faithfully give us the peace that passes understanding. Amen.

Fran Caffey Sandin is a wife, mother, grandmother, freelance writer, part-time nurse, and church organist from Greenville, Texas. She co-authored *Courage for the Chicken Hearted* and *Eggstra Courage for the Chicken Hearted* (Honor Books).

365 Reminders

Rebekah Montgomery

Fear thou not; for I am with thee: be not dismayed; for I am thy God: I will strengthen thee; yea, I will help thee; yea, I will uphold thee with the right hand of my righteousness.

Isaiah 41:10 KJV

I stood in our garage and opened the boxes of personal effects from my beloved Aunt Ruth, finding an old-fashioned birthday card. Inside, executed in beautiful penmanship, I found Isaiah 41:10. The card was signed "Momsie," my grandmother's pet name. A voice of gentle comfort from long ago echoed what I needed to hear that day. "*Fear thou not; for I am with thee*."

Many things were scaring me just then. My family had uprooted and moved so I could accept a wonderful job. Three months later, my "wonderful job" evaporated when the company was sold. My husband was unemployed and there was tension between us, our kids were having trouble adjusting to the new school and area, and a "neighbor" attempted to run over our youngest son, an adopted biracial child, and then painted a hate-filled epithet on our garage.

But the Lord had clearly spoken to me about making a career out of writing inspirational books.

Scared? Yes! *Dismayed?* Absolutely!

It was then that my aunt died and I found the birthday card and the verse inscribed on it by my grandmother. I didn't know what was going on in Aunt Ruth's life that prompted her mother to send those encouraging words, but I knew God's promise was meant for me, too. Adding a photo of Grandma and a bit of fancywork, I mounted the birthday card between two thin sheets of glass and keep it next to my computer where I can read the verse and be encouraged to live with confidence in God.

I've since discovered that 365 times in the Bible God says, "Fear not!"—one for every day of the year. It's become my personal challenge to ask daily, "What would I do for God today if I weren't afraid?"

Father, help me to boldly walk the paths that You have marked for me. Let me leave the world a better place because I have taken "fear not!" to be a command and trusted You enough to act on Your behalf.

Rebekah Montgomery has over thirty years of experience as a pastor/teacher. She is the author of six books and numerous periodical articles. Presently, she is writing *Fire Walking—Overcoming Fear with Faith.*

He Called Me by Name

Rose Sweet

"Fear not, for I have redeemed you; I have called you by your name: you are Mine."
Isaiah 43:1 NKJV

My childhood was noisy and fun-filled, with seven siblings and as many neighborhood kids in our home at one time. Our dinner table was an old, eight-foot door Dad had covered with colored ceramic tiles, and mealtime always included much children's chatter and cheese sandwiches.

On weekends, we'd pile into the family van and drive to church, filling a whole pew by ourselves. As the oldest, I loved being junior mom. I can still remember our babies' fresh-washed heads and sweet milk smell as I held them in my arms. My dream was to grow up, marry a man like Dad and, like Mom, have lots of little babies.

That was in the fifties.

In the nineties, I tragically found myself in my forties, divorced, and quite alone. I'd never had my own children, my parents were in nursing homes, and my brothers and sisters were scattered across the country. I was an odd number at parties and was too young to join widows' groups. Most single men my age had also been divorced and were too discouraged or too scared to try again. I didn't seem to fit anywhere.

Even at middle age I still wanted to be loved, to belong to someone, *anyone!* One night, before going out on yet another doomed blind date, I suddenly felt the Lord's Word wrap itself warmly around my heart. "*I have called you by your name: you are Mine.*" Even though I'd read it before, now I *felt* it. That was the last night of my deep loneliness. Sometimes I still struggle with having no family, but I know I am His. He has pursued me. He wants me. He'd do anything to have me. I am His beloved, and He is mine. He has called me, Rose, by name! I belong!

And never forget this: so do you!

Lord, whenever I feel alone or emotionally abandoned, please heal my emotions. Remind me of Your unfailing love. I praise You, I love You, I adore You. I am Yours.

Rose Sweet is a speaker, retreat director, facilitator of DivorceCare, CLASS graduate, and author of *A Woman's Guide: Healing the Heartbreak of Divorce.*

Princess for a Lifetime

Sheryl Pellatero

One thing I have desired of the LORD, *that will I seek: That I may dwell in the house of the* LORD *all the days of my life, to behold the beauty of the* LORD, *and to inquire in His temple.*

Psalm 27:4 NKJV

As a girl, I couldn't wait for my birthday. I dressed up in my best outfit and waited with much anticipation for my guests to arrive. I knew that when the door opened, my friends and family would enter my house to honor me.

They were coming to celebrate with me another year gone by and present me with gifts. I was the "princess" and the center of attention. Oh, how my heart was filled with great excitement and wistful expectancy.

I picture my Lord in the same way. He waits for me to open the door and step over the threshold to His throne room, His dwelling place. He sits patiently with great expectancy for me to arrive. He plans the celebration carefully. He looks forward to the gifts I will present Him, no matter how small they might be. He is the King and wants to be the center of my attention.

So, each day, I arrive and enter in. Each time I come near His throne, I see more of His beauty and glory. Sometimes I just kneel and worship, and other times I climb up on His lap and rest my weary head upon His shoulder. I find refuge under His wings from the storms of life.

Psalm 27:4 is my life verse. These words remind me what I need to do every day, all day—to come and dwell in the house of the Lord. This is where I will truly see God in all His glory. Then, and only then, can my Lord and I have complete and total oneness and truly awesome fellowship throughout the day.

Dear Lord, I bow my knees in worship and surrender.
Remind me daily that You await my presence
in Your home. Give me the strength to continue on in
intimate fellowship with You. In Jesus Name, Amen

Sheryl Pellatero lives with her husband and children. She is an active Bible study teacher, writer, and conference/retreat speaker. Sheryl is the founder and president of Solid Truth Ministries.

Surprise!

Leslie Vernick

I will give you the treasures of darkness, riches stored in secret places, so that you may know that I am the Lord, *the God of Israel, who summons you by name.*

Isaiah 45:3 NIV

I hate surprises. It's not that I hate being surprised; but when I know something good is coming, I hate to wait for it. My husband just can't understand why I read the end of a novel just to know what happens and then go back to finish the rest later.

When I was a little girl, I discovered (it wasn't by accident), some wrapped Christmas presents on a tall shelf in a dark hallway closet. I carefully unwrapped them one by one to see what they were and whom they were for. Many were for me. I was so excited; I could barely wait until Christmas to receive them. Unfortunately, when my mother realized that someone had been sneaking a peek at her hidden treasures, she was not happy. She threatened not to give me my gifts just because I saw them ahead of time.

Like my carefully hidden Christmas presents, often the treasures of God are concealed in the dark where we can't readily see them unless we diligently look for them. Diamonds don't hang from trees but are deep in the belly of the earth. They are plentiful and available but must be excavated out of that darkness in order to be seen and enjoyed.

As believers, we dread darkness because it usually symbolizes sin, depression, and that terrifying dark night of the soul. Doubt, despair, and feeling separated from God are often the emotions that accompany our interior nightfall. Yet, God promises us something wonderful in the midst of our darkest times. Like twinkling stars that shine the brightest on a black night, God offers us special secret treasures that remind us that He has not forgotten us and we are not alone.

Dear Lord, thank You that even in my darkest times You want me to know You are with me. Open my eyes to discover the riches that You have stored up for me. Show me where to find my treasures of darkness so that I might know You better and trust You more.

Leslie Vernick is a popular speaker and the author of several books including *How to Act Right When Your Spouse Acts Wrong.* Leslie loves teaching others how to move their faith from head knowledge to heartfelt trust.

Husband of the Scriptures

Sandra P. Aldrich

Your Maker is your husband—the Lord Almighty is his name—the Holy One of Israel is your Redeemer; he is called the God of all the earth.

Isaiah 54:5 NIV

When my husband died of brain cancer, I felt lost. How was I, a Kentucky woman, trained "to take care of a man and young-uns," going to raise two children alone? The worries seemed greater in the evenings; after I put our ten-year-old son, Jay, and eight-year-old daughter, Holly, to bed, I couldn't stand the thought of going back downstairs. In the past, after the kids were asleep, Don and I talked about the day's challenges, then dreamed about a better future. We'd even planned which colleges our babies would attend.

I faced the future alone. Each evening, I would tuck both children in, pray with them, and then go to my lonely bedroom. There I would read every grief book I could get my hands on—

all the way from clinical reports to the down-home experiences of others. But nothing eased the knot around my heart.

It was only when I set aside all the books and picked up the Bible that healing began. I turned to Philippians 4:19 KJV, *"But my God shall supply all your need according to his riches in glory by Christ Jesus."* Then I read Isaiah 54:5.

In the days ahead, that verse would help me make scary decisions. When I was offered a career change three years later that meant a move to New York. I started to panic over where we would live and where my children would go to school. One night I finally said, "Lord, husbands worry about housing and schooling. You're my husband; You figure it out. I'm going to sleep."

There were plenty of rough days ahead, but I learned to trust my Husband of the Scriptures, not only with my eternal life, but also with my day-to-day decision-making. And none of that would have come if I'd still been trying to glean strength from the grief experts.

Lord, thank You for hearing our heart's cries and for gently wiping our tears. Help us give our pain to You and trust Your presence in the days ahead.

Sandra P. Aldrich, president and CEO of Bold Words, Inc., is a popular speaker and author.

Poured Out . . . Yet Filled

Lucinda Secrest McDowell

If you spend yourselves in behalf of the hungry and satisfy the needs of the oppressed, then your light will rise in the darkness, and your night will become like the noonday. The Lord will guide you always; he will satisfy your needs in a sun-scorched land and will strengthen your frame. You will be like a well-watered garden, like a spring whose waters never fail.

Isaiah 58:10-11 NIV

"Well, I certainly feel poured out, Lord. In fact, I feel downright empty!" I muttered while packing for yet another speaking engagement. My week at home had been full of a myriad of family mini-crises, church involvement, plus the kids' school and sports activities. I was weary and worried. How could I possibly be used to minister to hundreds of women this weekend?

Over and over I kept reciting my "Life Verses"—Isaiah 58:10-11—which I'd chosen thirty years earlier when I was a college freshman. Strangely enough, God's words were even more relevant to me today; they were His promise that when I minister to others, He would satisfy, strengthen, and provide for me. Not only that, but also my own light would rise in the darkness.

How I longed to bring light and hope to women in the pain of darkness. But even with a ministry called Encouraging Words! I have to find that same encouragement daily—that Source—for my spiritual filling. You can't pour out if your own soul is empty!

Oswald Chambers reinforced this concept in his devotional, *My Utmost for His Highest*, "The process of being made broken bread and poured out wine means that you have to be the nourishment for other souls until they learn to feed on God."[2]

Taking a deep breath, I claimed, "Make me 'a spring whose *waters never fail.*' God, continue to fill me so that I may nourish others." I closed the suitcase, grabbed my airplane tickets, kissed my husband and daughter, and once again went forth with my small light against the darkness and a prayer on my lips.

Most gracious Heavenly Father, help me stay close to You so that I may pour myself out and truly be a never-ending spring, nourishing others with both Living Water and the Light of Life. Amen.

Lucinda Secrest McDowell, a graduate of Gordon-Conwell Seminary, shares hope and grace as a national conference speaker, author, pastor's wife, and mother through her Encouraging Words! ministry.

[2]Oswald Chambers, *My Utmost for His Highest* (Urhichsville, OH: Barbour Publishing., 1992), 28.

Choose the Ancient Paths

Cindi McMenamin

This is what the L*ORD says: "Stand at the crossroads and look; ask for the ancient paths, ask where the good way is, and walk in it, and you will find rest for your souls."*

Jeremiah 6:16 NIV

I stood at the crossroads all right. And I was badly in need of rest.

It had been a whirlwind month of speaking engagements, traveling, media interviews, and jet lag.

As I stood at the crossroads . . . in a sense . . . looking one way and then the other at the pace and direction my life could take, I found myself asking God for "the right way" and the strength to walk in it. I wanted that rest for my soul . . . and I had a feeling I needed to give up something in order to get it.

"Ask for the ancient paths," were the words that kept coming to mind.

"What is the ancient path, Lord?" I asked. "Is it the path that is pretty much covered up because it hasn't been traveled much lately? Is it the path that takes much longer to walk?"

Could it be the path Enoch took when he walked with God three hundred years? Could it be the path that Abraham took when God began calling him His friend? Is it the path of slowing down and walking with Him and talking with Him, as the world rushes by?

"Show me that ancient path, Lord," I prayed. "I do want to walk in it."

The next day I cancelled a few engagements on my calendar and set out to walk more slowly down a path less traveled. I planned less, prayed more, spent more time with my daughter, and began to learn what it meant to be still before God. And the peace and joy and true rest that followed were indescribable.

God knows what He's talking about when He hints about the "ancient paths." The question is this: Am I willing to stand apart from the rest of the world and walk it a bit slower in order to discover the precious peace and rest that await me on the way?

Lord, show me the ancient paths that lead straight to Your heart, and give me the determination to walk in them. I'm ready for the rest and refreshment that come from walking by Your side.

Cindi McMenamin is a pastor's wife, mother, national conference speaker, and author of the books *Heart Hunger* and *When Women Walk Alone*.

For I Know

Kari West

"I know the plans I have for you," says the Lord. "They are plans for good and not for evil, to give you a future and a hope."
Jeremiah 29:11 TLB

I wondered if I would ever climb out of the pit that first Christmas after my divorce. Since my daughter chose to visit her dad, I decided to travel to Israel with a group of her classmates and their parents. On New Year's Day we stopped for devotions in the hill country outside Jerusalem, just as the sun came up. Behind us was the bustling city, and far beyond our sight was the verdant Jordan Valley. I wedged myself between the rocks and remembered the words—*hinds' feet on high places* (2 Samuel 22:34; Habakkuk 3:19). Glancing at the steep slope below the roadway, I realized the peril of traversing this treacherous terrain. My trek that year through the landscape of grief had also been more rocky and perpendicular than smooth and straight.

As I opened my Bible, a card that I'd tucked inside tumbled out. "Please don't forget that the Lord has something perfect in store for you. Just concentrate on letting God's love heal you and get ready to handle His blessings," my friend Regina had written. I chuckled; I could barely manage the moments let alone imagine a future.

Perched on the jagged edge of a past that was no longer an option, I prayed for courage to face a new year and chose the words of Jeremiah not only as my verse for that year but as my life verse.

Fourteen years have passed since that pivotal moment. I now know that loss is simply the risk we take for living and loving . . . that there is a future beyond grief, but that hope requires a long view . . . that while we are longing to see our life back in order, God is longing to show us Himself.

Lord, in a topsy-turvy world where people get sick and die and not everyone keeps a promise, help me center my hope, my identity, and my security in You alone.

Kari West is an author and speaker living in Northern California with her new husband, two dogs, and a goat named Sigmund. Her latest book is *Dare to Trust, Dare to Hope Again: Living with Losses of the Heart.*

Just What I Was Looking For

Thelma Wells

Be anxious for nothing, but in everything by prayer and supplication, with thanksgiving, let your requests be made known to God; and the peace of God, which surpasses all understanding, will guard your hearts and minds through Christ Jesus.

Philippians 4:6-7 NKJV

In the early 1990s I asked God for a scripture that I could call on during the next twelve months. When I finished praying I turned on the television to hear a preacher. He said, "There's someone out there who wants to know what their scripture will be for this next year. Go get your Bible and turn to Philippians 4."

Hurriedly I got my Bible. The first couple verses were interesting. But when I got to verse 6 my eyes enlarged because I knew in my heart that was my scripture.

After discovering word meanings and committing those words to memory, I thought I was ready to stop worrying. But situations began to shatter my peace: getting stuck in airports, having to drive on icy roads only to learn that the program, to which I'd skidded hundreds of miles, was cancelled.

Later that year I experienced some interpersonal skill challenges. I became upset with people who hadn't been fair with me. A business deal fell through that I had counted on to supplement my finances. Health issues became pressures on my emotions. There were deadlines and extremely annoying time demands. In almost every case, I pressed the repeat button in my mind's computer and recalled that scripture . . . "be anxious for *no-thing!*"

It's been over a decade since that fateful day when the Holy Spirit answered my prayer for a sustaining Word. But almost every day I have had to remind either myself or someone else of those true and powerful words: "*And the peace of God, which surpasses all understanding, will guard your hearts* [that means your emotions] *and minds* [that means your intelligence] *through Christ Jesus.*"

Jesus, thank You for being the Prince of Peace. May we always remember that we can find peace when we keep our minds on You. Amen

---

Thelma Wells is a speaker, author, and president of A Woman of God Ministries. She is the founder of Mother of Zion Ministries, a speaker with Women of Faith, and a Professor at Master's Divinity School and Graduate School, Evansville, Indiana.

Eavesdropping

Sherry M. Jones

How priceless is your unfailing love! Both high and low among men find refuge in the shadow of your wings.

Psalm 36:7 NIV

I had just found the perfect spot near my front door for a large terracotta planter that overflowed with the most gorgeous, greenhouse-grown, purple geraniums. The newly sprouted aspen leaves whistled in the spring breeze as I heard a deep voice drawing nearer in the distance.

Intrigued by the unique echo of this weary but gentle-spirited traveler, I tipped the rim of my sun visor with my gardening gloves to catch a glimpse.

As I looked up, I saw a small entourage moving slowly, very slowly, across the street. The grandpa's words became clearer. "Come on, Michael, we're almost home. Don't dawdle. Let's go get some ice cream. Don't cry, Michael. Do you want Papa to carry you? Just a few more steps."

With the leash of the family's yellow Labrador in one hand, the loving grandpa took his free hand, reached down with his strong arm and picked up his bewildered eighteen-month-old grandson who'd just sat down on the neighbor's driveway in pure exhaustion. The little curly, blonde-headed twin sister didn't stop, but continued to lead the pack, as the grandpa cautioned, "Avery, honey, slow down, we need to wait for Michael. Come back here to Papa, honey. . . ."

Seeing these two free-spirited little children and the family dog being led by their loving Papa made me think of our walk with our Heavenly Father. He lets us exercise our free wills without much constraint. He gives us guidelines to follow and even picks us up and holds us when we fall. Sometimes, *like Avery*, we want to take control and get ahead of God's timing. Sometimes, *like Michael*, we don't think we can take one more step. We're frustrated, irritable, and don't think God is paying close attention to us. Yet our Abba Father is leading us as Papa led the dog to a wonderful place of refuge. He has exciting plans for us, if we'll wait on His timing, listen to His voice, and follow Him.

Dear Heavenly Father, thank You for Your loving-kindness.
Help us to keep our eyes on You and not on our circumstances.
We know Your plans for us exceed our highest expectations. Amen.

Sherry M. Jones is the author of *Broken, But Not Forgotten.*

Whatever Comes My Way

Carole Lewis

"I know the plans I have for you," declares the Lord,
"plans to prosper you and not to harm you,
plans to give you hope and a future."
Jeremiah 29:11 NIV

My husband Johnny was diagnosed with prostate cancer in October 1997. Since the cancer had spread to the pelvic bone we didn't have many treatment options. However, I claim Jeremiah 29:11 in my personal life. And God has blessed us mightily according to what He has said, and He has taught us to treasure every minute we have together. Without this problem we would have continued to take life for granted as we had for so many years. Cancer has made it very easy to know what our true priorities are and to follow after those things that are most important—God and family.

As the director of First Place, a nationally recognized Christian health program, I have quoted Jeremiah 29:11 many times during the last few years. As we sought the perfect new publisher for our program, God showed us time after time His wonderful plans for us.

As another example of how God has used this verse in my life, my eighty-eight-year-old mother has lived with us for the last year and a half. God has given me this opportunity to repay my mom, in some small part, for all the love and sacrifices she made for me. Through this experience God has shown me what real service is and how we are more like Christ each time we serve others.

Through this verse, God has mightily shown me that no matter what life brings my way, whether in my professional life or my personal life, He has good plans for me. His plan is to prosper me and not to harm me. His plan is to always give me hope and a future.

Father, help me remember each day the promise You made to me in Jeremiah 29:11. May I always look for Your plans, not mine. More than anything, I want to be Your woman. Knowing that I grow most when I am squeezed and stretched, I want to graciously embrace whatever You send my way. Teach me to know You and the power of Your resurrection.

Carole Lewis has served as the National Director of First Place, a Christian health program, since 1984.

An Audience of One

Sherrie Eldridge

When you were born, no one cared for you. When I first saw you, your umbilical cord was uncut, and you had been neither washed nor rubbed with salt nor clothed. No one had the slightest interest in you; no one pitied you or cared for you. On that day when you were born, you were dumped out into a field and left to die, unwanted. "But I came by and saw you there, covered with your own blood, and I said, 'Live! Thrive like a plant in the field!' And you did! You . . . became . . . a jewel among jewels."

Ezekiel 16:4-7 TLB

Losing my mother at birth left the inside of my heart a crater. You wouldn't know it to look at me, but I am a fifty-six-year-old woman who was adopted at ten days old and who had always looked at life through a lens of rejection.

My counselor said she didn't believe I'd gotten in touch with my unresolved grief and suggested I go to a local hospital and ask God to show me what I'd lost. I went into a neonatal unit and I looked long and hard at those precious ones. I prayed and prayed, but no lightning bolt of insight struck, nor were there any feelings of sadness.

On my way home, my body began to convulse with deep sobs. One phrase and a word came to mind. "On the day you were born" and "jewel." Once home, I rushed to my trusty concordance and found the words in a scripture. Through the tears I learned God validated my feelings of abandonment. He was there on the day I was born. He called me forth to life through a relationship with Him. He considered me His jewel.

That was His opinion of me! *His jewel!*

A sense of peace descended into my innermost being. I was a changed woman! To this day, I rarely struggle with self-esteem, for I am playing to an audience of One.

Oh Lord, thank You so much for healing my innermost being and revealing Your opinion of me. Knowing that I am Your jewel is all I need in this world.

Sherrie Eldridge is an internationally known speaker on the subject of adoption, the author of *Twenty Things Adopted Kids Wish Their Adoptive Parents Knew*, and the President of Jewel Among Jewels Adoption Network, Inc.

Distress Signal

Deb Haggerty

In my distress I called to the Lord, and he answered me.
Jonah 2:1 NIV

In *my* distress I called to the Lord, and He answered me.

The year 1999 had been tough. My father and father-in-law died, my business was not doing well, my husband traveled most of the time, and I was alone. Alone with my thoughts, worries, and fears, I struggled to endure from day to day.

In my *distress* I called to the Lord, and He answered me.

December 13, 1999. The technician at the mammography center was chirpy, "Ninety-five percent of the time the screening shows nothing." Irritated, I snarled. Out of the room she went to develop the films—the next thing I knew she was back, stern and serious. "We need to do more films."

In my distress I called to the Lord, and He *answered* me.

My doctor called before I got home from the center, wanting to see me.

"How attached are you to your breasts?" She asked.

Looking down, and then looking at her, I said, "Well, the last time I checked they weren't fastened on with Velcro!" She collapsed in laughter.

In my distress I called to the Lord, and He answered *me.*

The year 2000 was my journey down the path that so many women have trod, the path of cancer. Yet this time was one of the greatest blessings in my life. I received dozens of encouraging notes letting me know how much I was loved. Through e-mail I was able to share my journey and minister to others. I learned there was strength in weakness, comfort in being comforted. And I was victorious and will live victoriously until proven otherwise—God is so good!

Lord, remind us that You are with us always, in the valleys and on the mountaintops. Help us to listen to You and walk the paths You'd have us tread. Thank You, Lord, for answering me so richly.

Deb Haggerty is an author, speaker, and three-year breast cancer victor dedicated to encouraging others. She lives in Orlando, Florida, with her husband, Roy, and Cocoa the dog.

Though It Tarries . . . Wait

Georgia Shaffer

"Though it tarries, wait for it."
Habakkuk 2:3 NKJV

"Write a book," the still quiet voice said one morning as I wrote in my journal following the loss of my health, job, and marriage.

"Why would I write a book?" I argued. "English and writing were my worst subjects."

"Because it will help others," came the simple response. With those five words, I began the slow, painful project of learning how to write despite the doubts, which kept shouting, "Give up; you'll never succeed!"

And those doubts continued to scream for six years as I struggled to complete my first book proposal. But, it was my Habakkuk 2:3 that quietly encouraged me. It reminded me to wait and write, write and wait.

Ten years after God planted the seeds of that dream, I held my first published copy of *A Gift of Mourning Glories*. I thought about all the years of discouragement, the tears of frustration, the fears that it would never happen, and the words that helped me to press on.

It wasn't just getting a book contract that seemed to take forever. There was my long recovery after a bone marrow transplant for a recurrence of breast cancer. Month after month, year after year, there seemed to be little improvement in my strength and stamina. There was the five-year battle with the insurance company for the costs of the transplant (over $110,000). There were seemingly insurmountable obstacles we faced with my son's learning disabilities. Only when he and I looked back years later could we see any significant progress.

Oswald Chambers said, "One of the greatest stresses in life is the stress of waiting for God."[3] That is why, in the midst of our struggles and the apparent lack of progress, we need to remember that we must wait, even when success tarries.

Dear Jesus, too often we want instant success.
We don't like the pain that comes with long effortful tasks.
Help us to remember that waiting is part of the process.

Georgia Shaffer is a speaker, psychologist, and Christian Life Coach in Pennsylvania. Her book, *A Gift of Mourning Glories,* offers a practical approach for those facing changes they did not choose.

[3]Oswald Chambers, *My Utmost for His Highest: An Updated Edition in Today's Language,* James Reimann, Ed. (Grand Rapids, MI: Discovery House Publishers, 1992), February 22.

Thunderstruck

Kathy Blume

The Lord your God is in your midst, a victorious warrior.
He will exult over you with joy, He will be quiet in His love,
He will rejoice over you with shouts of joy.
Zephaniah 3:17 NASB

Life became painful . . . emotionally and physically. I had been a happy little girl until I was seven. Suddenly my world began to change. I was diagnosed with polio, and the small things in life took on infinite importance to me. I wasn't like the other kids anymore. I wore special shoes and had to sit alone in the house while the neighborhood children played, ran, and laughed outside. The hospital visits changed me, too, and seemed to forever seal the fate of the once happy little girl who would never be the same.

A few years ago, I discovered Zephaniah 3:17. It was one of those moments when I was thunderstruck by the living Word of God and His Holy Spirit. He was saying to me, "Kathy, I have loved you from the moment you were born and still love you intensely. I am a Father who rejoices over you every day. You are my precious daughter, and you must never forget what is in My heart toward you. Will you look to Me in the midst of any circumstance, no matter how painful, and remember this?"

Now, fifty year later, I have been diagnosed with post-polio syndrome. Victims of this disease experience a weakening of the muscles originally attacked by the virus. Sometimes the pain can be excruciating. Still, I rest in the assurance that I have a God who "exults over me with joy," who dances over me no matter what I think, feel, or accomplish for Him. And I am so grateful.

O Father, please forgive me when I concentrate on my circumstances and fail to remember how very much You love me. I especially love it when You not only sing over me, but when You sing to me. Amen

---

Kathy Blume and her husband Bob have a blended family with five married sons (four of whom are pastors) and eleven grandchildren.

Hope for the Future

Susan Titus Osborn

"I know the plans I have for you," declares the Lord, "plans to prosper you and not to harm you, plans to give you hope and a future."

Jeremiah 29:11 NIV

The darkest time in my life, 1987, I took a step of faith. A divorce after twenty-two years of marriage left me with a son in college and one in high school. I didn't have a college degree, and I hadn't worked in twenty years. I didn't have any idea how I could earn a living or provide for my boys, but I learned very quickly what it meant to step out in faith.

I got down on my knees and prayed, "Lord, can I make a living as a freelance writer and editor?" Although I was working only about five hours a week at my writing and five hours a week at Biola University, I felt the Lord encourage me to try.

He opened doors to writing books, setting up a critique service, and offering writing classes at Biola University, where I was already assistant director of what was then the largest Christian writers' conference in the country. Although I never knew from month to month how much money I would make, I was always able to pay my bills when they came due. God also provided a way for me to continue my education, obtaining a B.A. in Religious Studies and an M.A. in Communications.

Then, after five years as a single mom, I married Dick Osborn, who has encouraged me in my writing and editing to become all God wants me to be. Three different times during our ten-year marriage Dick has been out of work for periods of six months, eight months, and two years. Yet we have learned not to worry about finances. God truly does have plans to prosper us. He is our hope, and He always will provide for our future.

Dear Lord, we do not always know what the future holds. Yet You always do know. And You have made plans to provide for our needs and to give us hope. Thank You. Amen.

Susan Titus Osborn is director of the Christian Communicator Manuscript Critique Service. She is contributing editor of *The Christian Communicator* magazine and an adjunct professor. She has authored twenty-five books.

Seek First the Kingdom of God

Judy Hampton

"Seek first his kingdom and his righteousness, and all these things will be given to you as well."
Matthew 6:33 NIV

Excruciating pain came into my life in the form of a family crisis. No one had any answers for me. But my pain drew me to God's Word and I began to feed on it. The Word of God satisfied my hungry soul. It began to change *me*, and transform *me*.

Why? Because it's alive, and inspired, profitable for training in righteousness, so that we might be adequate in *Him*. (2 Timothy 3:16.) As I gained God's viewpoint, I learned that God wanted to use my trial to change *me*, and make me more like His Son. (Romans 8:29-31.) For the first several years of my Christian life I had wandered in the wilderness, feeding off the ineffective substitutes, instead of feeding on His Word. I settled for sermons, devotionals, and interesting books *about* God. As a result, I remained a baby Christian. I was biblically malnourished and had a wrong view of the Christian life.

Up until then, I thought life was all about me and getting my own way, and living a comfy, cozy Christian life. I was deceived. His Word never promises that.

As I sought Him first each day, I began to see His plan unfold. He wants to give us the power to live *above* our circumstances, and to reach a lost world with His message of salvation. That is why we so desperately need to seek Him first, with a surrendered heart. Then He'll give us the power to live differently. If we choose to seek ourselves first, we'll live *under* our circumstances.

As a result of crisis which sent me running to Him, I've found there is no sweeter place on earth than sitting at the feet of Jesus, learning from Him, and being transformed.

Father, give us a hunger to seek You first every single day. Give us hearts that desire to obey You and reach a lost world with the Gospel of Jesus Christ. We pray this in His strong name.

Judy Hampton is a keynote speaker for women's conferences across the United States. She is the author of *Under the Circumstances*.

The Resting Place

Julie Baker

"Come to me, all you who are weary and burdened, and I will give you rest. Take my yoke upon you and learn from me, for I am gentle and humble in heart, and you will find rest for your souls. For my yoke is easy and my burden is light."

Matthew 11:28-30 NIV

Most of us no longer live in an agricultural society; therefore, we may not readily see what the yoke symbolism in Matthew 11:28-30 illustrates. Years ago, I performed *The Resting Place*, a song I wrote based upon these verses. After the concert a weathered man greeted me.

"You know, young lady," he said as he offered me a knurled hand, "that was a beautiful song, but let me tell you what it means from an old farmer's point of view.

"You see, in the old days, I used to train a team of oxen to help me till the land. I would place the yoke around the neck of an older, more experienced ox, and pair him up with one of the younger ones. Now, the older ox knew my voice, my word commands, and what the movement of the reins meant. I would yoke him together with the less experienced oxen, which did not know the commands, or carry the weight of the plow.

"Jesus does that for us. When we are yoked together with Him, all we need to do is to walk beside Him. He carries the burden for us and knows the Master's commands so that by walking next to Him, we know the right path to follow."

It is no wonder, then, that when we are joined together with Jesus, His yoke is easy and His burden is light!

Heavenly Father, thank You for carrying the weight of my burdens and guiding me each step of the way. Help me to hear Your voice so that I can obey Your commands and walk close beside You.

Julie Baker is a recording artist and founder of the TimeOut for Women! conferences. She is the author of several books, including *A Pebble in the Pond: The Ripple Effect* and *Take Time for Prayer.*

Always

Dayle Allen Shockley

"Surely I am with you always."
Matthew 28:20 NIV

"O God, where are You? I need to know that You are here with me, in all of my turmoil and grief."

Filled with anxiety, I had stepped out into a cool October night, seeking solitude. The sky stretched over the yard like a dark, blue velvet cloth. I walked to the tall pine in the front yard and slumped down on the cold ground, pulling my legs close for warmth.

With my head between my knees, I prayed for relief from the circumstances that had plagued me for months.

My plea floated across the lawn and vanished into the night. I sat a moment longer, desperate for a word from the Lord. But there was only quiet. With a heavy sigh, I raised up and leaned back against the tree, the darkness seeming to swallow me up. And then something wonderful happened.

I opened my eyes, and there, in the heavens, surrounded by a deep blue sky, was what looked like the biggest diamond I have ever seen. As an enthusiastic observer of the heavenly bodies, I knew it was the magnificent Venus. Did you know that Venus, the most brilliant planet in the solar system, is both a morning and an evening star? Had I been sitting anywhere else in the yard, I would have missed this sight.

I shivered in the night air. I knew God was there, filling the vast space around me. I sensed that He was saying to one of His despondent children, *I really am here, dear child. Morning and evening—I will always be here.*

That was all I needed to know.

Dear Lord, when we feel we're all alone in our despair,
remind us to look up. Morning and evening
show us the reassuring signs of Your presence.

Dayle Shockley's work has appeared in numerous periodicals, including *Guideposts, Focus on the Family, Moody, Catholic Digest,* and *The Dallas Morning News.* She is the author of three books and is a writing instructor at a Houston college.

A Pony in Lace

Rebekah Montgomery

"Give, and it will be given to you.
A good measure . . . will be poured into your lap."
Luke 6:38 NIV

When I was a child, I wanted a pony. I read and dreamed about ponies. I even pretended the broom was a pony. I prayed so fervently for one that I'd race to the window afterwards, expecting to see a pony hock-deep in Queen Anne's lace, country breeze blowing its mane and tail.

I began to save my allowance in a jar under my bed. Then missionaries came showing slides of faraway children hearing the gospel for the first time. Although the children looked like smudges with white teeth, I was very moved. The missionary passed the offering plate. As I bowed my head to pray, I "saw" the jar under my bed.

A mighty internal struggle ensued. I slept little that night. Toward morning, I opened the jar, pouring out the coins: Five dollars, twenty cents. Chores, birthdays, allowance, pennies rescued from the gutter—all saved a cent at a time.

"It's Yours, Lord," I told Him.

At church, I poured the change into the offering plate. A penny bounced over the rim, hit the floor on edge, and rolled to the altar, as if it were anxious to present itself to the Lord.

I relinquished my pony dreams, saving halfheartedly. I wondered about the little children in Africa, hoping to introduce myself when we got to heaven. Maybe a pony would be tethered in the Queen Anne's lace outside my heavenly mansion.

Then Mother took me to visit my uncle who had a farm with ponies. I tried to make adult conversation with him.

"How much does a pony cost?" I asked.

Offhandedly, he remarked, "You want a pony? I'll give you one."

Within a month, a pony stood in our pasture, knee-deep in Queen Anne's lace, country breezes ruffling its mane and tail. For me, faith was the substance of ponies hoped for and the verification that God honors His promises with a ride of joy.

Father, all I will ever own is Yours, coming from Your hand. Help me to remember to freely give it back to You for safekeeping.

Rebekah Montgomery has over thirty years of experience as a pastor/teacher. A prolific writer, she is the author of several books. She lives in Illinois with her husband and children.

For So It Seemed Good

Brenda Poinsett

"I thank thee, O Father, Lord of heaven and earth, that thou hast hid these things from the wise and prudent, and hast revealed them unto babes: even so, Father; for so it seemed good in thy sight."

Luke 10:21 KJV

"I've been fired," my husband Bob announced.

"You've been *what?*" I couldn't believe it was happening again. Just fourteen months earlier Bob had been fired from his previous job. Immediately, a refrain started playing in my head: *I can't go through it again, I can't go through this again . . . .* The anxiousness, the uncertainty, and the stress of the first job loss were still fresh in my memory.

I knew Bob needed me to encourage him, but the words just wouldn't come. In the past, I would have expressed confidence in him, in God, and in the future; but I didn't see much of a future for us. Who would hire anyone fired twice in fourteen months?

Fortunately, my writing project at the time was the prayer life of Jesus. As I studied His prayers, I noticed a phrase He prayed on two different occasions. One was a happy occasion (Luke 10:17-21), and the other was a time of rejection (Matthew 11:20-26). As I worked on the manuscript, I was drawn like a magnet to *"For so it seemed good in thy sight."*

The words troubled me so I made them my prayer, and slowly my perspective changed. Perhaps in some deep, mysterious way God was accomplishing in our lives something I couldn't begin to fathom. I stopped saying, "I can't go through it again," and began to encourage Bob.

Bob eventually got another job—see, the situation wasn't hopeless!—but it wasn't the last "hopeless" situation. However, now I know I can change the way I feel. Praying Jesus' words ignites hope because I am reminded there's more to any situation than what I can see. In God's eyes what I label as impossible may very well be full of possibilities.

Thank You, Father, that my perspective isn't the only perspective.
Help me to remember to work at seeing my difficulties
with Your eyes so I will hope and not despair.

Brenda Poinsett, author of ten books including *Why Do I Feel This Way?*, works with women who want a new sense of belief in themselves.

Piecemeal

Patsy Clairmont

"Gather the pieces that are left over."

John 6:12 NIV

I realize feeding five thousand (John 6:8-13) with the lunch of one small boy was miraculous. Heaven knows I've wished for that kind of scenario when unexpected company dropped in at dinnertime and found us dining on last week's macaroni. Or when I underestimated the appetites of my crew and the banquet table was inhaled before folks had eaten their fill. Or when my new recipe turned out to be revolting (Turkey ala Fling).

But the incident in the story that caught my heart's attention was the weighty issue Jesus addressed after He fed His hungry followers. It was His treatment of the scraps, the leftovers, the broken pieces. I love when Jesus instructs His people to gather them up in baskets.

I have been a basket case most of my life in one way or another. As a teen I was a rebellious runaway. As a young married adult I was an agoraphobic, emotionally and physically housebound. As a mature (tee hee) woman I hit menopause early and it's stayed long and late (Yikes!). I have always felt emotionally piecemeal. So I am deeply comforted that Jesus values fragments.

Even though I am much more "together" than I was as a teenager, I still find myself falling apart over devastating losses, heartbreaking consequences, and personal storms that have wrecked havoc in my world. So I am learning (boy, am I slow!) that I will always need Jesus to gather me up. My human frailty, gratefully, I will shed when I reach glory, but until then I need Jesus to commission disciples to help carry me to Him.

Moses, the great Old Testament leader, started life off as a basket case. The Lord God sent Pharaoh's daughter to pluck that little Hebrew leftover out of the wicker to become a prophet, liberator, lawgiver, and historian. Hope for all basket cases!

Feel like a leftover? Broken? Scattered? There is One who values your life and longs to gather you to Himself.

*Lord, thank You that You use simple things like a child,
a lunch, and baskets to perform miracles. And bless
You for using fragmented lives for holy purposes. Amen.*

Patsy Clairmont spends her days reaching out to hurting women through her books, such as *Mending Your Heart,* and speaking at the Women of Faith conferences.

No One But Jesus

Eva Marie Everson

After this a lot of his disciples left. They no longer wanted to be associated with him. Then Jesus gave the Twelve their chance: "Do you also want to leave?" Peter replied, "Master, to whom would we go? You have the words of real life, eternal life. We've already committed ourselves, confident that you are the Holy One of God."

John 6:67-68 The Message

"You aren't going to believe this," my friend Donna* said from the other end of the phone. "Kari* has left the church."

I was stunned, stupefied even. "What do you mean? She's left our church or she's left the faith?"

"She's left the faith."

I stopped breathing; it felt as though there wasn't enough oxygen in the world to fill my lungs. How could that be? How could a woman of such extreme faith leave the very One she loved so intimately? Wasn't this the woman I had listened to, hour after hour, ministering to a hurting world around her? What hurt cut her so deeply as to make her walk away?

I was reminded of the scripture in John where Jesus told His followers they must eat of His flesh and drink of His blood. For any self-respecting Jew, these steps were too difficult; their law forbade them to partake of anything with blood in it. This new teaching seemed incomprehensible.

In our walk with God, we are often faced with difficult choices, steps, and times. There are days when we fall to our knees, crying out, "Jesus, I can't do this anymore!" But we choose to press forward because having known Him—having truly loved Him—we can't imagine life's moments without Him. Where else would we go? To whom would we turn?

I don't know what happened to Kari; after her decision to leave the church, she left her home and family. Though heart-sick, my own faith was reaffirmed and my soul moved closer to the One I love most.

Dear Jesus, we love and adore You. You have the words of eternal life. We embrace and trust them and remain committed to You. We love You, Father. We trust You, Jesus. Empower us, Holy Spirit. Amen and amen.

Eva Marie Everson's work includes *Summon the Shadows, Shadow of Dreams, True Love,* and *One True Vow.* She is a nationally recognized speaker and Bible teacher.

*Names changed.

Believing the Truth

Cynthia Spell Humbert

"You will know the truth, and the truth will set you free."

John 8:32 NIV

A good portion of my adult life has been spent believing things that weren't true. These lies weren't blatant or silly, like believing the world is flat or that Santa really does exist. (Even I can figure those things out!) No, these lies were more subtle and shame-based. I had practiced them for so long that they had begun to seem normal, a part of my everyday life.

Viewed simply, John 8:32 means that truth equals freedom and lies equal bondage. In my internal tape deck, I played messages such as, "You are so stupid!" "If anyone knew the things you've done or who you really are, they could never love you." "You must be perfect." "You need to have everyone's love and approval." My emotional and spiritual life was in constant turmoil, and I felt like a failure.

On the other hand, God desired to bring me truth and freedom in the inner parts of my being and thinking in order to produce healing changes. He longed to help me clean out the lies I believed, pull up the hidden roots of shame, and replace them with the gentle truth and assurance of His unconditional love for me.

Practicing the truth about how God views me healed hurts and banished the harmful lies that had me trapped. Until I identified the lies and replaced them with the truth, I could not find emotional and spiritual freedom.

Jesus said, *"I am the way, the truth, and the life. No one comes to the Father except through Me"* (John 14:6 NKJV). Wow! The Truth has been revealed to us through the Person of Jesus Christ! What a comfort to learn that the more intimate we become in our relationship with Jesus, the more we will know, understand, and live in the freedom His truth brings!

Father God, thank You that You know every detail of who I am, and yet You always pour out Your love and grace toward me. I am blessed to be Your daughter!

Cynthia Spell Humbert was a therapist with the Minirth-Meier Clinic and is the author of *Deceived By Shame, Desired By God.* Cynthia and her family live in Austin, Texas.

Passport to Abundance

Karen O'Connor

"I came that they may have and enjoy life, and have it in abundance (to the full, till it overflows)."

John 10:10 AMP

Visions of a new car, a house of our own, a vacation to an exotic island danced in my head. Some twenty years ago, John 10:10 appeared to be a passport to abundance when I was a new Christian in a new Bible study. At first I was very excited about it. But over the years since, the Lord has given me a deeper understanding of its meaning. There is nothing wrong with cars, houses, and vacations, but the word *fullness* means so much more than material prosperity.

Life in all its fullness encompasses *all* that life brings—the sorrows and the joys—including pain and grief, time in the valley and in the desert, as well as time in the meadow and on the mountaintop. The thief may come to steal and kill and destroy, but Jesus came to lay down His life for His people, so that even in the midst of challenge we can rest knowing He is with us in the *fullness*—He will never leave us nor forsake us. There is nothing outside of His providence, His plan, or His promises.

I also take comfort in belonging to a family of believers that spans the whole of biblical history! Their stories are mine, as well. The Old Testament Israelites, for example, lived on manna for forty years wandering in the desert. Then God brought them into a fruitful land all their own.

The disciples in the New Testament feared for their lives when the storm came up on the sea and rocked their fishing boat from side to side. But when the time was right—Jesus calmed the wind and the rain.

Again and again, He makes His purpose known—to give us "life in all its fullness." Our purpose, then, must be to *live* to the *fullest*—the life He gives.

Sweet Lord, You are the fullness of my life—my hope, my joy, my salvation. How blessed I am to be called Your child and to know that You are my provider, my refuge, and my strength.

Karen O'Connor is an award-winning author, popular retreat speaker, and a writing mentor whose mission is to inspire people toward greater intimacy with God, themselves, and others.

Lost Sheep

Virelle Kidder

"My sheep listen to my voice; I know them, and they follow me. I give them eternal life, and they shall never perish; no one can snatch them out of my hand."

John 10:27-28 NIV

My clothes were packed, Bible and notes by the front door. I laid out a favorite black and white woven jacket, black skirt and shoes, and searched for the treasured black and white porcelain sheep earrings my daughter had given me when she was in college. They were missing. Not in the jewelry box, not on the floor, nowhere in sight. Panicky, I tore through my closet, feeling the pockets of every robe and pair of slacks. Where on earth could they be? I could feel my heart pounding as the time for departure to speak at a Vermont retreat rapidly approached.

"Steve, have you seen my sheep earrings?" I called to my husband outside as he loaded the car. Reporting them missing for the second time was not an option. Bought at a great sacrifice, Lauren had once driven three hours to replace the first pair I had lost.

"No, but I'll keep looking," Steve volunteered patiently. "Just take your shower and don't worry."

Once in the shower, I cried out loud to God. "Lord, I can't find my sheep! I can't tell Lauren I lost another pair of earrings! Please, please, Lord, help me find my sheep!"

Gently, His voice spoke to my heart, "Virelle, I know just how you feel. I have lost sheep too. Will you help Me find Mine?"

"Oh, God, I am so sorry," I moaned and sniffed back my tears. I had forgotten why I was doing the retreat in the first place. Stilled, I whispered, "Yes, Lord, I'll help You find Yours." Just then, a loud knock came at the bathroom door. It was a jubilant Steve, sheep earrings in hand.

At the closing prayer of the retreat I shared the story of the lost earrings and God's tender words, offering anyone who found herself outside God's fold to come through Jesus, our Savior. Before I had said "Amen," a young woman whose silence had concerned me all weekend, leaped to the podium, placing both hands on my shoulders and cried, "I'm the sheep! I'm the one He sent you to call home!"

Father God, make me sensitive to the lost sheep around me. Touch my heart with the deep love You have for Your children who have not yet heard the voice of the Shepherd. Amen.

Virelle Kidder is a writer, conference speaker, and radio broadcaster from New York who has found great joy in sharing God's invitation to come home for over twenty years.

Happiness Beyond Boundaries

Christin Ditchfield

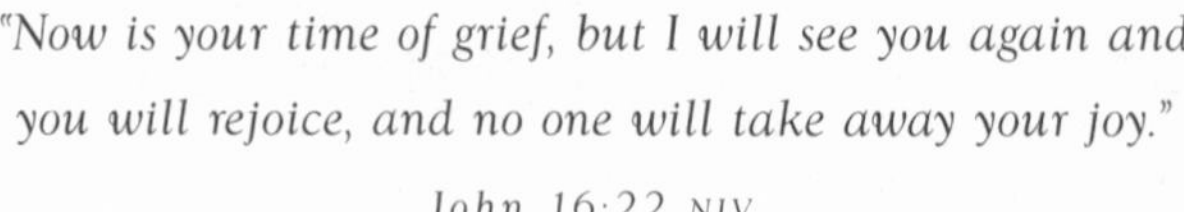

"Now is your time of grief, but I will see you again and you will rejoice, and no one will take away your joy."
John 16:22 NIV

I just love babies! I guess that's why I enjoy watching all those "Labor and Delivery" programs on the Discovery Channel. Having watched dozens of women give birth on these shows, I've noticed something. Every woman approaches labor differently. They use different breathing techniques and positions, different medications and therapies. Some are nervous or fearful; some get angry and upset. Most of them are in much pain. They may sob quietly or let out screams that would wake the dead.

But I notice in every case, the moment the baby is placed in the mother's arms, all her problems completely disappear. There is no more panic, no more frustration, no more pain. It's as if the events of the last 24—or 36—hours never even happened.

Mom's happiness knows no bounds. She doesn't regret a minute of the experience that enabled her to bring forth life!

Jesus talked about this in John 16:21-22, as He prepared His disciples for His death on the cross. He said: "A *woman giving birth to a child has pain because her time has come; but when her baby is born she forgets her anguish because of her joy . . . So* [it is] *with you. Now is your time of grief, but I will see you again and you will rejoice, and no one will take away your joy.*"

We live in a fallen world full of hurt, disappointment, and heartbreak. But the pain of this life is only temporary. Our suffering will not last. One day it will be completely forgotten in the joy we experience when Jesus comes back to take us home with Him. That's a joy that will last forever!

Lord, thank You for the hope of heaven and the joy it brings. Help me to make the most of the time You have given me here on earth, as I look forward to the promise of Your glorious return.

Christin Ditchfield is an author, conference speaker, and host of the nationally syndicated radio program, *Take It to Heart!*

The Giving Blessing

Ellie Kay

In everything I showed you that by working hard in this manner you must help the weak and remember the words of the Lord Jesus, that He Himself said, "It is more blessed to give than to receive."

Acts 20:35 NASB

One Saturday afternoon, after attending one of my coupon seminars, a lady named Cindy was traveling down Main Street in her small town. In her trunk, she had four bags of groceries for which she'd only paid *ten* dollars. As she stopped at a crosswalk for a mother with four young children, she noticed that the woman was blind. She watched the children push a rickety, metal cart which contained one small bag of groceries. Cindy assumed they'd just come from the corner supermarket.

In that moment, a still, small voice spoke to her heart and said, "*Stop your car and give them your groceries.*"

She'd *never* had any thoughts like this before.

Again, the thought came. "*Give them your groceries. It's your blessing to keep or refuse.*"

Cindy turned her car around and ran to the young family with groceries in her arms. As she placed the bags in the lady's metal cart she said, "I know you don't know me. That's not important. What *is* important is that God loves you and He wants you to have these."

The woman was bewildered and overcome by the kindness of a stranger. She didn't know what to do, as she stood on the sidewalk sobbing, "Oh, *thank you!*" As the children started rummaging through the bags, shouting, "Mama! There's fruit, cereal—and milk! We can have milk with our cereal." The youngest exclaimed, "Ders eben GUM!"

While Cindy was in the store earlier, using coupons to save money, God had a blind woman in mind. As *she* purchased gum, milk and juice, *He* was providing for four young children.

God's care for those in need is oftentimes manifested through us if we are willing to give lavishly. Just realize the incredible blessing that is tied up in this verse! When people share with others they discover that it is truly more blessed to give than to receive.

God, thank You for opening my eyes to see the needs of Your children and for giving the resources to be Your instrument of blessing to others in need.

Ellie Kay is the author of best-selling *Shop, Save, and Share* and *How To Save Money Every Day.*

Hidden Opportunities

T. Suzanne Eller

We know that all that happens to us is working for our good if we love God and are fitting into his plans.

Romans 8:28 TLB

I was fatigued, but I wasn't worried. After all, I was a busy 32-year-old working mother. Tired was my life! After a few weeks, I made a doctor's appointment. My world took on a whole new dimension that morning when the doctor said the word "cancer."

What followed was an incredible ten-year journey. Somewhere along the way God emerged in the midst of my dark and stormy circumstances and produced a silver lining called hidden opportunities. Who knew that battling cancer would give me the chance to share my faith, to kneel with unsaved loved ones, and to demonstrate the power of walking with God through hard times?

I'm certainly not alone. Many people in the Bible faced overwhelming obstacles. Philip and Andrew were asked to stretch a meager meal of five loaves and two fishes to feed a crowd of 5,000. Shadrach, Meshach, and Abed-Nego faced a fiery death sentence issued by an angry and jealous king.

What good could come from these challenges? The faith of the two disciples, Philip and Andrew, expanded every time they dipped into the meager lunch to feed the multitude. In the second story, the events that occurred in the fiery furnace brought a nation to its knees.

Yet, none of this would have happened if there had not been hurdles to overcome.

I admit it's hard to look for hidden opportunities when the flames are all you can see. But my battle with cancer allowed me to look at adversity in a little different light. When trouble comes, I have learned to ask, "What opportunity do You have for me now, God?"

With God's help, the perspective of our battles can be altered, helping us to see past the clouds and to reach for the silver lining of hidden opportunities.

Dear Father, thank You for the hidden opportunities in this battle and for the lives that will be touched. Thank You for walking through this with me.

Suzanne Eller is a speaker and author of *Real Teens, Real Stories, Real Life.* When not writing, Suzanne can be found riding horses.

Beauty for Ashes

Cheri Fuller

Therefore, I urge you, brothers, in view of God's mercy, to offer your bodies as living sacrifices, holy and pleasing to God—this is your spiritual act of worship.

Romans 12:1 NIV

The day of my mother's funeral, the sun rose brilliantly in the East Texas sky. I was exhausted from weeks at the hospital helping my mother before she died of cancer.

"Cheri, write down that little chorus, 'Beauty for Ashes' from Isaiah 61 you've been singing to me. If no one in our choir will sing it, I want you to promise me you will," Mama had said two weeks earlier.

I figured surely someone in the choir could sing the song; and besides, you don't argue with your mother when she's dying. But after she died, the pastor looked at Mama's directions and said no one in the choir knew the song or was willing to learn it on short notice.

"You'll have to sing it yourself or it won't be in the program," he said.

Just then I opened my Bible to that day's reading in Romans 12:1: "Present yourself . . . a living sacrifice." As I read, God's quiet whisper said, "Give yourself to Me as a living sacrifice, and I will do it through you."

As I got up in front of the sprays of yellow roses, mums, and gladiolas to sing "Beauty for Ashes" later that day, God did give me the grace and strength I needed.

Six years later when my first book was released and I began to speak publicly, I was petrified. *I didn't sign up to speak to big groups, Lord. It's too hard and I'm too scared. I just said I'd write this book and articles to encourage parents.*

"Remember what I showed you that morning of your mom's service? Give yourself to Me, and I will do it through you," the Spirit said.

He was right, of course. Jesus wants to live through us by His Spirit. He's just looking for willing vessels.

Lord, I give myself anew to You as a living sacrifice.
Use me, live through me, love others through me, and
accomplish Your purposes today as I yield to You.

Cheri Fuller is an inspirational speaker and award-winning author of thirty books, including the best-selling *When Mothers Pray.*

New Perspective

LeAnn Weiss

Even if it was written in Scripture long ago,
you can be sure it's written for us.
Romans 15:4 The Message

Growing up as a preacher's kid, reading my Bible was engrained in my daily routine from childhood. But as a busy young college student out on my own, I found myself trying to cram in my devotions the last few minutes before I'd fall asleep in the wee hours of the morning. The Bible seemed to have lost its relevance to my life, but I was going through the motions because I knew I should.

Then I started attending a new church that was practical and growing. One night, Pastor Loveless reflected, "I think the problem is that we've come to see the Bible as mere Sunday school lessons, instead of seeing it as God's love letter and timeless instruction manual for our lives."

He challenged, "Even if you start reading for only five minutes a day, don't just read the Bible as history, but as you read, ask the Holy Spirit to show you practical applications for your life and the lives of those you pray for, and start journaling what He tells you."

As I started reading God's Word following this challenge, the Bible came alive to me. Verses I had read hundreds of times before now had new meaning, in light of my present circumstances. Writing down the practical insights God showed me, my devotions became the highlight of my day.

One night as I read, Romans 15:4 seemed to leap off the page. I realized that I had associated the Bible more with rules than as a primary source of encouragement and hope.

Years of meditating on the Bible with an "encouragement filter" has totally transformed my personal relationship with God and opened ministry doors beyond my wildest dreams. I've learned that nothing compares to the encouragement found in the pages of God's Word.

Father, thanks for the awesome love letter You've written to me through Your eternal Word. Forgive me for the times I've treated Your Scripture as a mere history lesson. Let Your Word be my primary source of encouragement and hope.

LeAnn Weiss founded Encouragement Company in 1994. Her personalized paraphrased Scriptures are featured in the best-selling *Hugs* and *Heartlifters* series as well as *Good Things Come in Small Packages,* calendars, and greeting cards.

The Powerful and the Weak

Linda Evans Shepherd

God chose the foolish things of the world to shame the wise;
God chose the weak things of the world to shame the strong.
1 Corinthians 1:27 NIV

The senator's face was pinched with bitterness. "The lives of handicapped people are not viable," she told the subcommittee meeting in the state capital. "The handicapped cannot contribute to society and, in fact, they monopolize valuable medical resources."

Her words shocked me. *Not viable?*

I thought of Laura, my own disabled daughter, and realized that the hate I saw etched on the face of this powerful politician was actually directed towards persons like my own child.

Soon it was my turn to testify. I held my daughter's picture, knowing many would find it pitiful.

"You see, my daughter was the victim of a violent car cash," I explained. "She's paralyzed from the neck down, she's partially blind, and she's on life support."

The senator sighed in disgust, but I held her eyes with my own. "And it's true that Laura uses medical resources. But her life is wonderful. My daughter is full of joy and she knows no heartache. She gives and receives love freely. That's important because the number one command that Jesus gave us was to love God with all our heart and to love our neighbor as ourselves. My daughter does that better than anyone I know. Her life is viable indeed."

Later, in my daughter's room, I pulled my Bible open to one of my favorite passages, 1 Corinthians 1:27.

I closed my Bible and thought of the angry senator who had forgotten how to love and I had to wonder whose life—the powerful senator's or that of my handicapped child's—best reflected God's glory. The answer came simply. It came reflected in my daughter's smile.

Dear Lord, I rejoice that I am weak and You are strong.
For I am just the kind of person You can use!
Help my life be one filled with Your love and grace.

Linda Evans Shepherd, besides being a best-selling author and international speaker, is the mother of two wonderful teenagers, Laura and Jimmy. They reside in Longmont, Colorado.

Perfect Peace?

Karol Ladd

Thou wilt keep him in perfect peace, whose mind is stayed on thee: because he trusteth in thee.

Isaiah 26:3 KJV

Perfect peace? With laundry and phone calls and taking kids to practice? All too often I feel overwhelmed with a host of responsibilities and schedules to keep.

So what is "perfect peace"? Is it a euphoric state of mind that comes only from sitting on the beach, watching the gentle waves roll in? Or could "perfect peace" be described as a noiseless home, no phone calls, e-mails, or TV (like that's really going to happen)? Maybe perfect peace represents the time when the kids are not arguing.

Brother Lawrence, a 17th century kitchen worker, found perfect peace while he washed dishes in a busy Parisian monastery. He learned to practice the presence of God within mundane activities of life. Brother Lawrence chose to focus on God and worship Him throughout the day, no matter what he was doing. He truly "set his heart on things above."

It was worth a try. I began to practice God's presence in the midst of my most frazzled moments. Sitting in rush-hour traffic, I decided that instead of whining and stewing, I would worship and pray. I turned the eyes of my heart heavenward. There on the highway, true peace entered my heart as I recognized the warm embrace of the God of peace. I began to see the people in the cars around me as a part of His creation and prayed for their hurts and needs.

Another frazzled moment in my life turned into peace as I was standing in the slowest checkout line at the grocery store. There I began to thank God for His blessings and the means with which to make my purchases. I began to pray for the angry woman ahead of me and for the frustrated cashier. Although I wasn't in a tranquil setting, I had sincere peace.

True peace doesn't wait for the perfect circumstances; we experience peace as we focus on a perfect God.

God of peace, thank You for the peace You provide amidst the storms of life. Your peace is perfect; it passes human comprehension. How glad I am that I can come to You, anytime day or night, and You hear my prayer. I love You, Lord. In Jesus name I pray. Amen.

Karol Ladd is the author of twelve books including *The Power of a Positive Woman.* She is an enthusiastic speaker with a powerful and encouraging message.

Nothing Besides You

Cindi McMenamin

Whom have I in heaven but you?
And earth has nothing I desire besides you.
Psalm 73:25 NIV

Oh, to be so in love with Jesus that everything this world offers loses its appeal altogether! That was the heart and mind that Asaph, an Old Testament songwriter, had when he penned these words so long ago. And yet they hold such power over me today as I continually come back to them and do a heart check: "Cindi, what is the one thing you desire more than anything else? A better marriage? A child who loves and serves the Lord? A bigger, more effective ministry? A way to accomplish your dream and calling?"

As good as some of those things are, I realize they are not enough. They are not, in and of themselves, the prize. They have never satisfied. And they never will. That one thing I desire above anything else must be Jesus—all that He is and all that He has to offer. And when I am able to say that, perhaps all those other things will fall into place like wrappings on the prize.

Whom have I in heaven, supporting me, sustaining me, and shaping me into the woman who will one day see the face of God? *You, O Lord. Only You.* And what else on this earth can save me, satisfy me, and sanctify me for Your purposes? *Nothing, Lord. Only You.*

As I get just a glimpse of God now, and taste of His unfailing love, and see all that He is doing to make me into whom He designed me to be, how can I ever go back and desire something other than Him?

O Lord, fill that hunger in my heart for You alone. Be the only One exalted in my life so that I can honestly say, "This earth has nothing I desire besides You."

Cindi McMenamin is a pastor's wife, mother, national conference speaker, and author of the books, *Heart Hunger* and *When Women Walk Alone*.

The Greatest of These

Teresa Bell Kindred

Now these three remain: faith, hope and love.
But the greatest of these is love.
1 Corinthians 13:13 NIV

Mama had just turned fifty when we learned she was dying of cancer. When I was a child she had read 1 Corinthians 13, the love chapter, to me, but it wasn't until I saw that love demonstrated in my dying mother that I understood the meaning and power of love.

My husband and I had small children, but we lived close by and I was able to spend time with her every day. Her health deteriorated; she gave up her career, but she never complained.

One of her dreams was to take her grandchildren to Disney World even though her doctors doubted she'd have the strength. We did go, but she was too weak to walk. So I pushed her in a wheelchair while the children skipped ahead. When we came to the Swiss Family Tree House she asked me to stop;

then she pushed herself up and walked through the tree house, right behind my young son.

One month later Mama died. Flowers and plants filled the funeral home. Cards and letters from former students flooded our mailbox. Neighbors and friends brought food and shared my grief. All the seeds of love she planted over the years had multiplied and grown in the hearts of all who knew her.

Eleven years have passed. Our oldest son, whom Mama followed through the tree house, graduates from high school this spring. Rachel is junior class president and in charge of her prom. Even though I cannot share these things with Mama, I can still feel her love. It is wrapped around me like a warm blanket on a cool autumn night.

God was always the source of Mama's strength; I just didn't realize how strongly she depended on Him until she became ill. He gave her the courage to walk through the valley of the shadow of death without fear. He gave her love so powerful, it will extend through future generations.

Heavenly Father, I thank You for the gift of Your love, a love so great that You sent Your only Son to die on the cross for sinners like me. Help me to reflect that love so that others can see it and glorify You. In Your Son's precious and holy name I pray. Amen.

Teresa Bell Kindred is the author of two books, and she is a public speaker.

And the Comfort Overflows

D e b   H a g g e r t y

Praise be to the God and Father of our Lord Jesus Christ, the Father of compassion and the God of all comfort, who comforts us in all our troubles, so that we can comfort those in any trouble with the comfort we ourselves have received from God. For just as the sufferings of Christ flow over into our lives, so also through Christ our comfort overflows.

2 Corinthians 1:3-5 NIV

". . . who comforts us in all our troubles."

What a blessing this was to me! I really needed comfort. After seasons of trying, we'd accepted that getting pregnant was apparently impossible for us. I reveled in the verse—and let the "God of all comfort" comfort me. I took an assignment in the baby nursery at church where I could get the "baby fix" I needed and be of service too. Finally my heart was eased and I was at peace.

Then God taught me the rest of the verse: "*So that we can comfort those in any trouble with the comfort we ourselves have received from God."* A woman in the church was also having difficulty conceiving, and she was literally driving herself crazy. Somehow, she and I became friends and I was able to comfort her. And praise to Him, after she became contented with her situation, she became pregnant and now has two boys to grace her life.

I'd often thought of this verse—and the situations that flowed from it—when it became oh so relevant again. I was diagnosed with breast cancer. My friends comforted me and put my name on their prayer chains. The number of people who e-mailed to say they were praying or who just offered words of encouragement blessed me. I started writing "Updates from Deb" to keep everyone in touch with what was going on. And the comfort became comfort for others. The e-mail updates were forwarded to others who had friends or relatives with breast cancer. One of the e-mails I received said, "My mother has breast cancer. She is two weeks behind you and has been terrified. Since reading your updates, she is no longer afraid as you explained what happens so clearly." Many other similar notes followed—and the comfort truly overflows!

Father, thank You for being Abba Father, the Daddy whose arms we can run to when we need comfort.

Deb Haggerty is an author, speaker, and three-year breast cancer victor dedicated to encouraging others. She lives in Orlando, Florida, with her husband, Roy, and Cocoa the dog.

He Is at Work

Julie Ann Barnhill

In the Messiah, in Christ, God leads us from place to place in one perpetual victory parade. Through us, he brings knowledge of Christ. Everywhere we go, people breathe in the exquisite fragrance. Because of Christ, we give off a sweet scent rising to God, which is recognized by those on the way of salvation—an aroma redolent with life.

2 Corinthians 2:14-16 The Message

It's springtime in Illinois . . . finally. A mother robin can be seen from our foyer window, lounging sleepily upon the turquoise-hued eggs beneath her. The call of a blue jay is answered in kind as five kittens playfully romp on a back porch step. Spring . . . a cacophony of sights and smells. And, oh, what delicious smells! Lilacs wafting through a raised window. The intoxicating blend of an approaching rainstorm with the subtle hint of flowering peonies. The sweet aroma of budding trees, blooming hedges, and perennials peeking from the dormant earth—all testify to the Creator's fragrant and compelling handiwork.

Second Corinthians 2:14-16 has assured me over and over again of this truth: Christ is at work in me, always. When I'm standing in line at the local grocery, checkbook in hand and telling my six-year old "No" for the fifteenth time, Christ is at work.

After a day of speaking, as I'm slumped against an elevator wall and barely able to muster a polite smile to those around me, He is at work.

Second Corinthians 2:14-16 shouts to all of us who get caught in the mire of schedules and thinking that we have to be doing (active tense) something for God, 24/7, "Quit *trying* so hard!"

And then, when at last we are quiet, 2 Corinthians 2:14-16 whispers, "Rest, sweet one, rest. For I am at work in you, always."

Lord Jesus Christ, may men and women, boys and girls, be drawn, supernaturally drawn, to the intoxicating aroma of Your presence in us. Draw them by Your power to the life-changing and eternally sweet aroma of life that is found in You.

Julie Ann Barnhill is a speaker and published author. Her quirky sense of humor, dead-on delivery, and ability to connect humor with the heart, challenge and encourage her audiences.

God Allows U-Turns

Allison Gappa Bottke

Therefore, if anyone is in Christ, he is a new creation;
the old has gone, the new has come!
2 Corinthians 5:17 NIV

For thirty-five years I didn't believe in God. Thankfully, He never stopped believing in me.

I'd given up on God long before I ran away at fifteen to marry a man who went from being the love of my life to being my abuser, jailer, kidnapper, rapist, and attempted murderer. By the time I turned "sweet sixteen," I'd given birth to my son, divorced, and returned to school. There was no doubt in my mind—if God existed He certainly wasn't in my world.

There wasn't room in my life for a higher power greater than myself—I bought the New Age lies, certain I could "do it my way." For years, I filled my days with take-charge tasks, always on the move, always following a list. I filled my nights with alcohol, drugs, and self-destruction. I filled my soul with empty promises and emptier pursuits.

Why couldn't I find happiness? The feelings of utter helplessness and despair overwhelmed me. For years I was an angry, lonely woman, looking for love "in all of the wrong places." Doing things my way only sent me down dead-end roads.

How we come through times of struggle often depends on our level of faith and hope, and for years I had neither. It wasn't until Jesus Christ became real to me—when at last I admitted I couldn't do it on my own—that my life took on new meaning. The old truly did become new, and as Christ became my navigator, my life changed.

My U-Turn toward God began with 2 Corinthians 5:17. My path has gone from one of constant searching to one of peace and direction. This road map for living is available to anyone who will reach out and accept God's saving grace. Our God is a God of second chances and new beginnings.

You can never be so lost or so broken that you cannot turn toward God!

Lord, please give me the wisdom and strength to turn around and walk a path that will bring me closer to You. I want the old to be gone and the new to come. Help me to be all that You intend me to be. Amen.

Allison Gappa Bottke is the creator of the popular *God Allows U-Turns* book series.

His Strength, Not My Own

T. Suzanne Eller

When I am weak, then I am strong.

2 Corinthians 12:10 NIV

One man dead, three teenagers broken and battered. It was senseless, the death and grisly destruction of that night. My son's body was shattered in thirteen places from the waist down. The drunk driver didn't realize he would end his life and destroy my son's dreams the night he passed out behind the wheel of his car, veering head-on into the boys.

Weeks before the wreck, Ryan ran like the wind at state finals in the 800-meter event. Now after six weeks in the hospital, he was sent home in a wheelchair. He agonized through intense physical rehabilitation. I rejoiced in his first shaky steps and cried the day I realized he could no longer run with ease.

The bathroom was the only place I wept openly, for strength was my shield in the company of my son. But somehow, despite my façade, I knew I had lost something precious—not my love for Christ, nor my belief in God, but the ever-present strength that had been as close as a whisper. I struggled with anger over the stupidity of the driver yet mourned the loss of his life. Because of the man's lack of adequate insurance, I was left to fight discouragement over the thousands of dollars in medical bills. I felt weak and torn. I thought I had somehow let God down in my struggle.

"What has happened to me? I was the strong one, God. The one that encourages others," I cried out to God. These words were whispered in my heart: "When I am weak, then I am strong." Trusting my own strength was not sufficient.

True faith came in trusting God to carry me through the dark places and into the light.

Thank You, Lord, for the times You tenderly carry us through the difficult paths. Thank You for guiding us over the rocks and hills of life and for Your sufficient strength.

Suzanne Eller is a speaker and author of *Real Teens, Real Stories, Real Life.* When not writing, Suzanne can be found riding horses. Ryan now plays basketball and plans to major in pre-physical therapy in an Oklahoma university.

Life Verse

Jeanne Zornes

I have been crucified with Christ; it is no longer I who live, but Christ who lives in me; and the life I now live in the flesh I live by faith in the Son of God, who loved me and gave himself for me.

Galatians 2:20 RSV

The deadline to choose a "life verse" loomed for all of us in the church's youth instruction class. We would take a church doctrine test and quote a verse we'd want to carry through life.

I leafed through the Bible I'd gotten for perfect attendance in Sunday school a few years earlier. Its black faux leather cover had splitting seams and the red-edged pages were dimpled from rain. Here and there I'd underlined verses or scribbled sermon notes in the margins. Psalms held some possibilities. I skipped over the prophets and scanned through the Gospels. The Sermon on the Mount had candidates. But nothing grabbed me.

I flipped a few more pages to Galatians. Chapter two was riddled with my notes about how faith, not works, made me right with God, a message that turned upside-down my old version of Christianity. Weaned on the Ten Commandments and all sorts of family and school rules, I once thought getting to heaven meant hoping you were "good enough." Now here came Paul's letter to the Galatians. Across two millennia, the apostle showed me that Jesus' death was more than a Bible story. It was the fulcrum of history, God reaching down to man through Jesus Christ. God letting Jesus take my punishment for sin. God showing me a new way to live—not by my own power, but "crucified with Christ." I ended my verse search, choosing verse 20.

Like a snip of ivy, this verse is planted in my heart. For the past forty years, it's grown and entwined itself in my life. Whenever I am tempted to live on a merit system, God takes me back to that verse and to the Cross.

"Christ lives in me"—this is a verse with real life!

Lord Jesus, I claim the truth that You are living within me. Thank You for dying for my sins so I can live in the hope of eternal life.

Jeanne Zornes, Wenatchee, Washington, speaks and writes through Apple of His Eye Ministries. A wife and mother of teenagers, she's written seven books including *Spiritual Spandex for the Outstretched Soul.*

Immeasurably More

Nancy Kennedy

Now to him who is able to do immeasurably
more than all we ask or imagine, according to
his power that is at work within us, to him be glory.
Ephesians 3:20-21 NIV

My husband fell into a deep depression the same year I wrote *When He Doesn't Believe*. His depression took me by surprise because Barry has always been carefree and even-tempered. It felt as if the gates of hell opened up and dumped on our family.

At the time, Barry worked and lived out of town. His visits and phone calls grew less frequent. He talked about increasing his life insurance and what I should do "if anything happened." He said he wanted me to find a different husband, a Christian husband. He said he loved me and wanted more for me than he could offer. Then he said we should get divorced.

My world crashed. Barry and I had had our differences in twenty-seven years of marriage, especially after I became a

Christian, but he'd always been supportive. His talk about divorce came out of nowhere.

Throughout the years of praying for Barry to come to know the Savior, many times I've grown discouraged. In those times, the Lord comforted and encouraged me with Ephesians 3:20. I would stumble upon it in a magazine article or hear it in a sermon or testimony and know it was God's way of telling me not to give up; that He's not done yet and that the end result will be so much more than I could ever dream possible.

During Barry's depression (and, yes, it ended and the suggestions of divorce ceased), God "sent" me that scriptural reminder nearly every day in some form or another. Although other scriptures kept me from despair, Ephesians 3:20 was and continues to be a healing salve from God's heart to my wounded one.

Even though Barry's not yet a Christian, I don't despair because I know that God is able to do immeasurably more than all I could ever ask or imagine or even dream possible.

Father, thank You for Your very personal words of hope and encouragement to my often doubting heart whenever I need it most. You are indeed able and I am amazed. Amen.

Nancy Kennedy is the author of *When He Doesn't Believe* and *Move Over, Victoria—I Know the Real Secret.* She is also an editor and feature writer for the Citrus County *Chronicle* in Crystal River, Florida.

What I Am Becoming

Kari West

How precious to me are your thoughts, O God!
How vast is the sum of them! Were I to count them,
they would outnumber the grains of sand.
Psalm 139:17-18 NIV

"I like what we're becoming," my husband said. Richard's shoulder nudged mine as we strolled along the Pacific shoreline. Several steps ahead, Melanie, my daughter from my first marriage, and the dogs skipped through salty surf. We had come here for lots of reasons—to soak up sunshine on this unusually warm Thanksgiving, to let go of past memories, and to create new ones.

Seagulls swooped and squawked above us. I stuck my bare feet into the sand, digging toes into scattered clumps of broken shells and odd pieces of what once was whole. Crouching for a closer look, I combed the grains for an intact shell, but found none.

A jogger whizzed past. I stood up. To my right were two college-age girls heading up the bluff. An elderly couple, arms entwined, walked their dog several feet ahead. A middle-aged man sat alone reading a book. Several teenagers were busy tossing a Frisbee. A young mom unwrapped sandwiches for her toddlers.

Glancing at the trail of footprints and paw prints, I understood a truth that had eluded me before. The Creator sees my life not as odd pieces, scattered clumps, or crushed parts of what once was whole, but as a wide, wonderful beach engraved with His own footprints. My worth is not defined by success or failure, joy or sorrow, marriage or divorce. They are just part of the picture.

In that moment I realized that divorce, by forcing me to the end of myself, opened me to a world of possibilities much larger than myself. Life's journey is ongoing. The losses in my life are not wasted particles but an immeasurable part of the woman I am becoming.

Never forget what God thinks of you.

Lord, I'm tired of limiting my worth to others' definitions.
Help me see my life from Your perspective—
that I am still becoming who You created me to be.

Kari West is an author and speaker living in Northern California with her new husband, two dogs, and a goat named Sigmund. Her latest book is *Dare to Trust, Dare to Hope Again: Living with Losses of the Heart.*

How Do You Spell Relief?

Pamela Stephens

Do not be anxious about anything, but in everything, by prayer and petition, with thanksgiving, present your requests to God. And the peace of God, which transcends all understanding, will guard your hearts and your minds in Christ Jesus.

Philippians 4:6-7 NIV

My friend and I had just walked into the kitchen from outside when my five-year-old daughter Jenny interrupted our conversation, showing me a "sore" on her neck. I called our doctor immediately. After describing what I saw, he told me she'd be fine over the weekend. On Monday morning, however, we met the doctor at his office; he was amazed at her condition, and walked her across the street to the hospital.

The diagnosis was Stevens-Johnson Syndrome. Confused, my husband and I were in tears. We watched as they donned hospital gowns and masks and placed Jenny in "reverse isolation" so that the now-exposed raw skin would not become infected by any of us. They treated her by soaking her four times a day in saline solution (salt). Every time they came in to soak Jenny, she would plead with me not to let them. There was nothing I could do, other than feel helpless and out of control.

The following day, as I walked into the hallway, I remembered Philippians 4:6-7. I recall saying to God, "How can I *not* be anxious over this little child's situation? Please heal her . . . but if You choose not to . . . help me!" Even though I was so distressed at that moment, as I prayed I began to feel relief. A weight was lifted from me.

I felt just like a teapot turned on high! I began churning, bubbling, and finally whistling sweet praises. I was helpless as we carried Jenny into that hospital and during the first two days of her treatment. But when I prayed, I felt the pressure fade, replaced by the peace of God. Just as one of my favorite verses declares, "The peace of God, which passes all human understanding, shall guard your hearts and minds in Christ Jesus and give you peace." Prayer relieves pressure; it's as close as the next whisper of His name.

Dear Lord, thank You that You are a God who not only is in control of my life but in that of my children's lives as well. Help me to remember to always come to You to relieve the pressure that can build up in our hearts as we struggle to live for You.

Pamela Stephens has been married for thirty-four years and has two grown daughters and two grandsons. She enjoys speaking for women's retreats and other events and shares how God has taught her many valuable lessons through her life's experiences.

Whatever the Circumstance

Gayle Roper

I am not saying this because I am in need, for I have learned to be content whatever the circumstances.

Philippians 4:11 NIV

I was fifteen, the only Christian in my family, when I discovered, "*For I have learned to be content whatever the circumstances.*" It was this scripture that kept me from being bitter and resentful about feeling so alone, whether at church where all the other kids were with their families or at home where no one thought about life as I now did.

When I was twenty-six and, because of cancer, learned I would never be able to have children, this verse again came to my rescue. There would never be anyone who looked like me. Yet God was in charge of all my circumstances, even when they were painful. My responsibility was to *learn* to be content, to *learn* to accept His choices for my life with grace and thanksgiving.

At one point professionally I went through a five-year span of no sales. None. The only things that kept me going were seeing some reprints of articles and working with writers' conferences. All the new manuscripts I sent out were returned rejected. Again the idea of learning to be content *whatever the circumstance* was God's challenge to me. I am by nature ambitious, and the apparent failure of my call to write was bruising.

Of course I am content with the blessings God sends—a wonderful husband, two great adopted sons, two beautiful daughters-in-law, five absolutely amazing grandchildren, gracious friends, and an encouraging church. It's when the script doesn't go as I would have written it that I have "to learn to be content whatever."

As each book is released, as each speech is given, as each day is lived, it always comes back to agreeing with God that He and what He has provided for me are sufficient for His purposes for me. I continually learn and relearn to be content whatever.

Lord, when life isn't as we'd like, when hurtful things happen,
when we wonder what in the world You are doing,
teach us to learn to be content in the whatever of You.

Gayle Roper is the award-winning author of over thirty books.
Her most recent are *Riding the Waves* and *Spring Rain.*
She speaks at women's events and teaches writing across the country.

All Things

Janet Holm McHenry

I can do all things through Him who strengthens me.

Philippians 4:13 NASB

Many years ago I started a fifth-year teaching program, so I could become a high school English teacher with credentials. I had been out of college for more than sixteen years and had to take several national exams, one of which was particularly hard; I would be required to know authors' and characters' names, titles of novels and poems, etc. I'd never been very good at remembering things like that and I hadn't looked at them since college!

I was petrified enough to study for two solid months. I bought a book five inches thick that listed all the summaries of the major literary works and memorized titles, names, and plots until those fictional works filled my dreams. But still I wasn't sure I'd pass.

One morning while I was stewing about this, I heard a knock on the door. It was Roxanne, a casual acquaintance. She said, "I was driving by your house, and the Lord told me to stop and pray with you. Are you worried about something?"

When I could close my dropped-open jaw, I told her about the test, and she proceeded to pray through Philippians 4:13, over and over again, each time emphasizing a new word. By the time she finished—a half hour or more later—I was convinced I would pass the test.

And I did, with a pretty good score! I've been convinced ever since—as I teach, speak, or write—that *"I can do all things through Him who strengthens me."*

Lord, thank You that we can face
any challenge with the help of Your Son,
who gives us strength. In Jesus' name, amen!

Janet Holm McHenry is a speaker and the author of sixteen books including *PrayerWalk* and *Daily PrayerWalk*. She recently prayed through Philippians 4:13 again while recovering from back surgery.

Peanut Butter and Prayer

Sue Augustine

My God shall supply all your need according to His riches in glory by Christ Jesus.

Philippians 4:19 NKJV

With nothing left to eat but peanut butter and crackers, my little girls and I anxiously awaited my paycheck due to come in the mail on Friday. As a single mom, I depended on this money to buy groceries. When I found out there would be a delay because of our recent change of address, I was devastated. We knew we could count on family or church friends, but instead we decided to pray for a miracle. Although we ate peanut butter for every meal that weekend, we told no one of our need, becoming more and more excited about what God would do.

Imagine how overwhelmed we were to find our car full of boxes of groceries after church on Sunday morning! On each box was written, "God Bless You," and the verse, Philippians 4:19.

As we drove home, the girls teased me that, with all my tears before we even made it home, I would use up the two boxes of tissues that were included. Unpacking the groceries, we noticed the items and brands were exactly what we would have chosen. Our cupboards were full and, like manna from heaven, we seemed to have a never-ending supply.

Some time later we found out about the wonderful couple in our church who'd been obedient to God. During an evening church service, they'd both seen an image of my children and me, plus a dollar figure. After sharing their experience with each other, they asked God to reveal the meaning. It became clear that they were to purchase groceries of that dollar value and place them in my car two weeks from Sunday. They trusted the Holy Spirit to show them what to purchase and the bill came to the exact amount. God used these kind people as His instruments. Amazing how He looks after our needs before we even know we have them!

Lord, thank You that You are aware of our every need even before we are. Please help me to trust You fully and let me look only to You.

Sue Augustine is an international conference speaker, author of *With Wings, There Are No Barriers, 101 Innocent Pleasures,* and contributor to *Chicken Soup for the Soul.*

In All Circumstances

Susan Wilson

Do not worry about anything. Talk to God about everything. Thank him for what you have. Ask him for what you need. Then God will give you peace, a peace which is too wonderful to understand. That peace will keep your hearts and minds safe as you trust in Christ Jesus.

Philippians 4:6-7 BWE

My mother died on Good Friday 1993. Mother's life was an extraordinary example. One of her favorite guiding quotes was, "The classiest person is the one who makes the least number of people uncomfortable." So, when she died, I honored her example. I didn't cry; I didn't grieve; I helped others.

Three years later grief made its entrance. Depression wrapped its ugly arms around me. For months, during my morning time with God, tears engulfed me. Aching, wracking sobs. Then my family would wake up. I'd quickly dry my eyes, buck up, and get my family out the door. Repeatedly, through the day and without warning, fresh tears flowed uncontrollably. I couldn't escape my sorrow.

One morning while on my knees sobbing once again, I experienced God's voice. "Put Me at the center of your world. Put Me at the center instead of your mother; then you will begin to heal."

I worked on that obedience and God was right. The healing began. The dark thoughts were fewer. The heaving, wracking sobs eased. But my sorrow and loneliness were still so big. I couldn't seem to shake my loneliness and my plea of, "If only Mother could be here." In my anger, I still demanded to know, "O God, why did You take Mother away?"

Then a friend who lives an incredible example of thankfulness and gratitude began reminding me that God directs us to *give thanks in all circumstances*. Slowly and with growing conviction I learned to say and then believe my words, "Thank You, God, for Mother's home with You. Thank You for Mother's life with Jesus. Thank You for bringing me to a point where I don't want her back with me. I know that she is happiest with You."

I find life is increasingly joyful when I remember to focus on thankfulness, the very lesson I've pushed my children toward for years.

Dear God, convict our spirits to give thanks in all circumstances. With gratitude, we glorify You as the Way, the Truth, and the Life. We praise You for Your sovereignty. Amen.

Susan Wilson loves God and wants that relationship to grow deeper and wider.

Every Minute, Every Day

Karol Ladd

Pray without ceasing.

1 Thessalonians 5:17 NKJV

As a young girl, I grew to love 1 Thessalonians 5:17, though probably for the wrong reasons. In my fourth grade Sunday school class I received a sticker by my name for every verse I memorized. "Jesus wept" and "Pray without ceasing" were my favorite verses. Of course I wasn't quite sure what "ceasing" meant, but it was definitely an easy verse to memorize.

Now I love 1 Thessalonians 5:17 for a different reason.

When I become a mother, I learned the necessity of praying continually. Never stop praying! Not only do I pray in a special time alone with just God and me in the wee morning hours, but I also love to continue praying throughout the day. I have found that praying throughout the day has changed me as a person.

Instead of grumbling about making my kids' lunches for the next day, I pray for them while I spread peanut butter and jelly. I pray for their lunchtime companions. I pray for their schoolwork and their understanding of the lessons. I pray for their teachers. I pray for their conversations with other students.

There are other times when I enjoy continual prayer. How wonderful to enjoy God's sweet fellowship as I wait in the line at the grocery store and pray for the people in the line around me. Little do they know of the spiritual action taking place on their behalf. What fun! I find great joy in praying while I fold laundry, which until recently was my most detested chore. There is eternal pleasure and peace when we keep our minds stayed on God and His work throughout the day.

As I pray without ceasing, I am actually practicing His presence all day long. There is no greater joy in life than to cast my cares and worries on Him and keep my eyes on the eternal picture through prayer. Amazing how a three-word verse can transform an attitude . . . and a life!

Faithful Father, thank You for providing perfect peace, even when chaos surrounds us. Produce peace in me as I abide in You. May our minds be stayed on You each day.

Karol Ladd is the author of twelve books including *The Power of a Positive Woman.* She is an enthusiastic speaker with a powerful and encouraging message.

Learning to Overcome

Leslie Vernick

Do not be overcome by evil, but overcome evil with good.

Romans 12:21 NIV

What can you say to a person who cries, "Why did God allow my father to rape me?" In my counseling practice I see the horrendous effects of evil in people's lives and relationships. Evil wounds the soul and destroys lives. Sometimes when my clients tell me about the evil done to them I struggle trusting the sovereignty and goodness of God.

Walking alongside such deep pain, I can become overwhelmed with the wretchedness of humankind and I am tempted to lose my way.

Each day the evidence of evil in our world confronts us. We can't turn on the television or read the newspaper without being assaulted with the threat of terrorist bombs, chemical warfare, murders, muggings, rapes, and abuses of all kinds.

This verse gives me tremendous hope and a battle plan so that I will not get lost. It shows me how this war with evil is to be won. It is not won by wielding the world's weapons for warfare. Those may curtail evil for a season but they will never overcome it. When Satan hurls evil our way, he not only wants to injure us, he wants to destroy us. Don't let him.

When evil hurts us, our human impulse is to strike back recklessly, but God shows us how to fight back righteously. "Overcome" is a fighting word. The good that is powerful enough to overcome evil only comes from Him. God gives us His weapons, the weapons of righteousness (2 Corinthians 6:7), that are strong enough and powerful enough to overcome and demolish even the toughest of evil's strongholds.

Jesus, help me in my fight against evil. Sometimes life is so cruel,
and I struggle with hatred, bitterness, and unforgiveness.
Teach me how to overcome evil Your way. With good!

Leslie Vernick is a popular speaker and the author of several books including her newest *Courageous Humility*. Leslie loves teaching others how to move their faith from head knowledge to heart trust.

The Brightest Light

Sharon Hoffman

Faithful is he that calleth you, who also will do it.

1 Thessalonians 5:24 KJV

There I was, a seasoned public speaker of twenty-five years, standing in the wings of the huge platform where I was to speak momentarily. Worried about my tripping over miles of taped microphone cords, I waited for my turn. In the weeks preceding this evening, I could hardly wait to deliver the inspirational message I knew God wanted me to share for this particular conference with an audience of several thousand women.

When the moment came, however, I was surprised to feel very much alone and very afraid.

No notes.

No podium.

Just that blinding spotlight.

My heart was pretty unsettled as I stumbled through the layering of stage curtains to clip the microphone on my lapel. I needed a promise from God to quiet my nerves. Instinctively, I prayed, "God, please help me. All I can see are bright lights, no faces. Usually the smiles and faces of the crowd help me to engage with my audience. I don't see any women's faces out there. I see only that blinding light. Help me to meet this challenge!"

In that brief moment waiting in the wings, His answer was clear and calmed my anxious heart.

Had God called me to speak for Him? Yes! Would He do it through me if I'd just let Him? Yes! In His grace, God brought the promise of 1 Thessalonians 5:24 to light.

I relaxed. All the pressure was off. God was faithful to "do it" for me. I was ecstatic! How like God to go way over the top. My message to the women went beautifully, and the feedback was very affirming. I'm so grateful for the promise that, no matter what, when God calls us to be used as His instrument, He is faithful. If we show up, He does the rest.

Father, please help me not to serve You in my own capabilities, but in total dependence upon You . . . I long to be used of You. I know You have called me to serve You and I trust You, my God, with the results.

Sharon Hoffman is impacting women's lives around the world as a speaker, author, and the founder of GIFTed Women—Godly Influencers for Today. She lives in North Carolina where her husband pastors.

A Steadfast Mind

Margaret Johnson

You will keep him in perfect peace, whose mind
is stayed on You, because he trusts in You.
Isaiah 26:3 NKJV

Many powerful scriptures have sustained me through the years, but one above all has upheld me through heartbreak and loss: Isaiah 26:3.

One of my earliest memories is of a framed scripture verse hanging on our kitchen wall. I couldn't know then how this promise would provide me with strength to carry on through troubled times. One translation reads like this: "God will keep in perfect peace all those whose mind is stayed on Him, because they trust in Him."

A steadfast mind! A mind stayed on God! This became my refuge on a fateful September morning when a telephone call brought the news that every parent fears. An auto accident had claimed the life of our vivacious eighteen-year-old daughter, Kathi. I leaned hard on this promise through times of deep grief.

Later, our only other daughter was abandoned by her husband of ten years, leaving her to complete her education and raise two small boys. Once more, my refuge for peace was in staying my mind on God's faithfulness to provide for our daughter and two grandsons. She eventually remarried a loving, supportive man and my thoughts relaxed.

Another September! Another telephone call. Our daughter brokenly whispered the news: cancer, that awful invader and wrecker of dreams. Not a cancer that could crawl into remission, but a rare form of incurable blood cancer. My prayers became anguished. "Oh, no, Lord, not again. Please don't take another daughter from us."

She journeyed through chemotherapy, radiation, and unrelenting tumors and into an uncertain future as I became shaky in my faith. Our daughter reminded me of my oft-quoted verse as we witnessed her faith grow strong.

It is true. As my mind is steadfastly stayed on God—as I trust in Him—He is faithful to His promises and blankets me with His perfect peace.

Lord, You are a promise keeper. You give grace, as the burdens grow greater. Thank You for Your unfailing love and perfect peace.

Margaret Johnson is the author of the best-selling *18, No Time To Waste* and ten other nonfiction and fiction books. She and her husband divide their time between Michigan and Southern California.

Dreams Come True

Sue Rhodes Dodd

Delight yourself in the LORD *and he will give you the desires of your heart.*

Psalm 37:4 NIV

"Lord, take these dreams away; it hurts too much to hope for them anymore."

How often I have prayed that prayer. Dreams are often desires of the heart, and visionaries with high hopes can experience devastating discouragement.

I was furious with God after my first marriage ended in divorce. "The one really big thing I ask You for, and You won't give it!" For months I fumed at Him for His "refusal" to save my marriage. My heart was crushed.

Then I'd look into the dark brown eyes of my little girl, marveling at how I did get one dream: to be a mother. Though only a baby, my daughter taught me much about joy, love, and laughter during a season when my heart ached. Rocking her to sleep every night, I prayed, "Father, send her a daddy and send me a husband. In the meantime, You've got to be both."

I have made Psalm 37:4 a lifetime prayer. When I earnestly seek the Lord, He takes good care of my dreams and me. If desires are not His best, He lessens their appeal; with time, they simply fade away. When my desires match His will for my life, I have to trust Him to bring them about at the right time and in the best way.

Ten years after my divorce, God brought the right man into my life. I appreciated my new husband as the treasured gift he was because I'd waited so long. We printed this scripture on our wedding invitation, and daily I discover more reasons why God made us His perfect match. My husband tells me a second chance at marriage and fatherhood has healed his heart too. And my daughter now has a dad she respects and adores.

I'm glad God answered my prayers *His* way.

Father, I surrender my heart's desires to You.
Take away ones not from You; fulfill Your dreams in me.
I choose to love and worship You with all my heart, and
I trust You with all my dreams. In Jesus' name, amen.

Sue Rhodes Dodd is pursing several lifelong dreams—singing, writing, and homemaking—in Tulsa, Oklahoma. She owns an editorial business, Amethyst Enterprises, and enjoys teaching, speaking, and offering others hope.

A Faithful God

Rebecca Barlow Jordan

The one who calls you is faithful and he will do it.
1 Thessalonians 5:24 NIV

"That's suicide to your ministry!" friends said when Larry resigned a pastorate with no other prospects in mind. *Where would we go?*

Surprisingly, that question bothered other people more than it did us. It wasn't the *where* or even the *how* that frightened me. What surfaced in my heart was a big *what?*

When Larry suggested ever so gently, "You may need to work for a while," my hidden fears floated to the surface as reality sank to the bottom of my heart. *What* would I do? What *could* I do? Yes, I had worked outside my home before children. But skills were limited, and I longed to stay at home and continue to pursue my God-given call to write.

Upon leaving, our accumulated vacation and sabbatical pay equaled two months' salary. God gave me a peace, but there were times when I was tempted to pray, *You do know what*

You're doing, don't You, Lord? My heart confirmed that God was faithful—but it was time to test His Word and what I claimed to believe.

We have petitioned the Lord often in our ministry, and God answers, but His answer is not always in our timetable. But this time God chose to bless a struggling family and answer far beyond what we could ask or imagine or hope. Two days after our eight-week pay ended, Larry started his new job as associate pastor two thousand miles away.

A few weeks before our move, I received a phone call from a publishing company offering me some assignments I could do at home—in the same town where Larry's ministry opportunity "happened" to open up.

Not only had God called us to His work, He had indeed been faithful to "do it."

Father, Your faithfulness overwhelms me. When You ask me to do something for You, You always provide the strength and the resources for the task. How can I thank You enough?

Rebecca Barlow Jordan, a speaker and best-selling author, has written of God's faithfulness in over 1600 inspirational works and numerous books including *At Home in My Heart* and *Daily in Your Presence.*

My Prayer Pal and Mentor

Charlotte Adelsperger

Oh, how kind our Lord was, for he showed me how to trust him and become full of the love of Christ Jesus.

1 Timothy 1:14 TLB

I shall never forget Laura Richmond, our children's preschool teacher, who brought about such joy in the "little school" in her home. Laura glowed with love and enthusiasm. It didn't take long to discover that she steeped her life in Christ and covered her steps with prayer.

Every Monday evening Laura hosted a Bible study for us young mothers. Soon we experienced wonderful "spiritual growth spurts."

Laura and I became close friends. She was a vibrant sixty, and I was in my thirties. Sometimes after preschool, we'd have lunch. We talked often about Christ's impact on our lives. And we'd laugh a lot. Laura became my spiritual mentor.

One day Laura and I discussed 1Timothy 1:14. As prayer pals we agreed to pray that affirmation for each other. We paraphrased it: "Thank You, Lord, for teaching (name) to trust You and for filling her with the love of Christ Jesus."

Then on Mother's Day an early phone call brought crushing news. Laura had been killed instantly in a car accident the day before. An intoxicated driver had smashed into her car. I shook and sobbed. I had lost one of the most "invincible" and beloved Christian persons I had ever known!

In spite of great sorrow the mothers' group met the very next evening. We read scriptures that Laura loved and choked out our thoughts. Immediately I recalled "our prayer verse" from Timothy. It brought a powerful new meaning—to trust God and to carry on the faith. Our group closed with tearful song, but God's presence enveloped us all.

O God, thank You for opportunities to grow with other Christians. Thank You for how Your living Word can be integrated into our lives as a reservoir of wisdom and strength. Through Christ. Amen.

Charlotte Adelsperger, author and speaker from Kansas, believes prayer pals can experience some of God's most precious blessings. She co-authored *Through the Generations: The Unique Call of Motherhood* with daughter Karen Hayse.

Whatsoever You Desire

Cristine Bolley

Delight yourself also in the Lord, and He will give you the desires and secret petitions of your heart.

Psalm 37:4 AMP

My appetite for more of God had been spoiled by cravings for more time. But God pursued me again by sending Evangelist Dick Mills to remind me of Psalm 37:4, which had stirred my teenage heart many years before, saying, "Cris, the Lord is giving you your heart's desires because you have delighted in Him. Loved ones who have not been interested in spiritual things will be inspired by the glory of God on your life."

Stunned by what should have been good news, I regretted that I had no passionate or noble desires beyond the life I already enjoyed. The following Sunday, a woman I barely knew approached me after church and placed a small tube of lipstick in my hand, saying, "I want to give this to you," then she turned to leave.

"Wait!" I pleaded, "This is my favorite color and brand! I haven't bought it in years because it's so expensive, but I thought about it just yesterday! Why are you giving this to me?"

"It was in my heart to do so," she said and then hurried out the door.

I knew I held more than a tube of lipstick; God had placed this key in my hand to unlock His greater truth. This gift proved God knew my secret petitions, and I suddenly feared the Lord in a way I had not comprehended before.

Later, when alone, I wept with gratitude for His intimate attention and prayed, "Lord, You are giving me my heart's desires, no matter how small or great they are! Let me not waste this grace! Cleanse my heart of vain, selfish desires and create in me a passion for world-changing influence. Let me crave what You crave, Father—I desire a heart like Yours!"

And so He said, "Then simply delight in Me."

Lord, Your Word says that by the fruit of my lips I am filled with good things as surely as the work of my hands reward me (Proverbs 12:14). I will extol You, LORD, at all times; Your praise will always be on my lips (Psalm 34:1 NIV), for there is nothing that I desire besides You (Psalm 73:25.)

Cristine Bolley's recent books include *Under His Wings—What I Learned from God While Watching Birds*, *Stories for the Spirit-filled Believer*, and *A Gift from St. Nicholas.*

Forever Perfect

Betty Southard

By that one offering he made forever perfect in the sight of God all those whom he is making holy.

Hebrews 10:14 TLB

For years I struggled with poor self-esteem. I had grown up believing that who I was depended on what I did. My church background had led me to believe good Christians were defined by the services they performed as well as by the choices they made and the life they lived. I tried very hard to live up to the ideals that had been proclaimed. Most of the time, from my perspective, I failed.

One day, during my daily devotions (part of doing the "right thing"), I came upon Hebrew 10:14. The Holy Spirit spoke to me very clearly, informing me that I was never going to reach that pinnacle of perfection by anything that I did. The scales fell off my eyes, and I realized for the first time, internally, that which I had been taught externally. Christ died for me and by His death and resurrection I had been saved from trying to be perfect in order to please Him. My part was to accept His gift, surrender my life to Him, and then cooperate with Him as He continues to work in my heart and life. I realized because of my acceptance of Christ's sacrifice that I became instantly perfect in the sight of God. I also realized that the job of making me holy was going to be an ongoing, lifelong job, entrusted to Christ through the power of the Holy Spirit.

It was a turning point in my Christian life. I began to respond to God out of a grateful heart and what I did became a joy rather than a burden. Now my self-esteem comes not from what I do but from what He has done for me.

Father, help me to see and understand that You are
the only one who can make me holy, and then
help me to hear and obey Your voice and direction.

Betty Southard is a speaker, author of *The Grandmother Book, Come As You Are,* and *The Mentor Quest,* teacher for Christian Leaders, Authors, Speakers Seminars, and Minister of Caring for the Crystal Cathedral's *Hour of Power.*

His Heart to Mine

Debbie Alsdorf

"Before I formed you in the womb I knew you,
before you were born I set you apart."
Jeremiah 1:5 NIV

As a small child I often felt invisible and alone. Everyone around me was either busy or tired. I wondered *who* I was and if I mattered. I began to define who I was by the opinions, expectations, and the approval (or disapproval) of others. I worked hard at recognition through accomplishments and consequently began to run the wheel of performance and perfection.

Those who have worked hard at approval through achievement know the endless trap of always having to *be better.* The problem with this kind of living is that our focus gets fixed on people and their expectations of us, rather than on the God who created us for His purposes. By pleasing people we learn to live in fear rather than in the freedom that God has for us.

There is a peace in embracing the truth that the same God who made the sun, the moon, and the stars formed me in my mother's womb and from that time has set me apart for His plans. I don't have to perform, achieve, or do anything significant to be noticed or loved by Him. Instead I am free to move about with the heartbeat of God.

There are many verses that touch my heartstrings and stir hope within me. But, the verses that touch me most deeply are those, like Jeremiah 1:5, that speak of God's involvement in my life. It's amazing to think that God set me apart as a piece of His divine plan from the beginning of time.

Being noticed or approved by others becomes less important when I believe that Almighty God knows me, loves me, and has always planned for me. With that truth in my heart, I live differently.

Father, in You I have found my purpose for living. I trust that You haven't forgotten me or Your plans for my life—not even for a moment. I place the "me" that You know inside and out, into Your hands once again, saying, "You know me well."

Debbie Alsdorf is a speaker and the author of *Steadfast Love, Living Love,* and *Restoring Love*. She currently serves on the pastoral staff at Cornerstone Fellowship in Livermore, California, as the director of women's ministries.

His Unfailing Love

Donna Partow

"So now I have sworn not to be angry with you, never to rebuke you again. Though the mountains be shaken and the hills be removed, yet my unfailing love for you will not be shaken nor my covenant of peace be removed," says the Lord, who has compassion on you.

Isaiah 54:9-10 NIV

I don't like to admit this, but I'm disappointed with my children on a fairly routine basis. They do dumb stuff. They break things. They run the other direction when I stand on the deck yelling, "Dinner!"

I used to worry that God was the same kind of parent: disappointed and frustrated with His misbehaving children, of whom I am surely the chief. Indeed, I seem to possess an uncanny ability to "snatch defeat from the jaws of victory."

Several years ago, I managed to embroil myself in yet another mess-of-my-own-making and was sure my Heavenly Father was going to sever all parental ties. I spent an entire Saturday crying out to God, fearful that He was going to say to me what I've said to my children on occasion: "*This* time you've really done it!" Finally, I collapsed in exhaustion. The last words I muttered were: "God, are You angry with me?"

The next morning, sitting in church, my eyes fell upon my open Bible. The passage leaped to my rescue: "*So now I have sworn not to be angry with you.*" I was overwhelmed with the love of God. He was never more real, more personal, to me than at that moment. I have never loved Him more. As I've allowed the words of this passage to seep into my soul and spirit, they've transformed me from the inside out. God isn't an angry, disappointed parent. He's not sitting in heaven waiting for me to slip up. I don't need to live in fear anymore. God has made a covenant of peace with me, sealed in the blood of Jesus. He has compassion on His children, because He made us and knows our weakness.

Nothing can shake His unfailing love for His children.

Lord, I thank You that even when the obstacles in my life seem like mountains, Your love for me cannot be shaken. I'm thankful for the realization that hardships are not a punishment but a time to draw closer to You.

Donna Partow has authored ten books, including the international best-seller, *Becoming a Vessel God Can Use*. She's been on over 200 radio and TV programs, including *Focus on the Family*.

Wisdom Grantor

Brenda Nixon

If any of you lacks wisdom, he should ask God, who gives generously to all without finding fault, and it will be given to him.

James 1:5 NIV

Five years ago I faced an unexpected option. A major surgical procedure would give incredible relief to a health problem. However, I dreaded the familiar pain from an operation. My doctor said that we could wait, he didn't think it was immediately required. Undecided, my husband and I took the dilemma to God. "Can You give wisdom for or against surgery now?" we asked Him.

"But I can wait," I argued, not wanting to do something rash and irreversible.

We sensed an urgency to proceed. Knowing God gives wisdom, we told the doctor to make plans. Insurance approved the surgery in record time. Within weeks of what usually takes months I was in pre-op. Sharing one last prayer with my pastor, I found myself whimpering, "Surgery is so serious. I sure hope this is the right choice."

Days later the doctor strolled into my hospital room. "The operation took three hours," he announced. Wide-eyed I listened as he explained, "It was more difficult than I predicted. We did the right thing to do it now because it would have been more serious if we had waited!" Warm tears of relief rolled down my face as I recognized the wisdom of God and His guidance.

James 1:5 has always soothed me. It assures me that the only perfect Parent recognizes the shortcoming of His children and gives generously when asked for help. He does not lecture, condemn, or make us wait while He thinks about it, nor find fault with us for needing to ask. He responds liberally.

I'm grateful for a receptive Father who welcomes my requests, knowing there will be times I'll need heavenly wisdom for future earthly decisions.

My confidence is in You, Heavenly Father.
Only You see the future. Grant me wisdom to make
the right decision when I don't know what to do.

As a speaker/writer on parenting, Brenda Nixon is devoted to building stronger families. She is author of *Parenting Power in the Early Years*.

Perfect Gift

Shirley Rose

Every good gift and every perfect gift is from above, and comes down from the Father of lights, with whom there is no variation or shadow of turning.
James 1:17 NKJV

My childhood was fairly happy, but it was a huge heartbreak that my parents didn't know the Lord. I could attend church only because a neighbor faithfully gave me rides.

I knew there weren't many Christians in our extended family. My paternal grandfather was a minister, but he was killed in an auto accident before I was born. I lived out of state and never knew my grandmother well. Because God was such a huge part of my life, I always felt a little cheated that I didn't have a strong Christian heritage.

Through a peculiar set of circumstances, I met an elderly gentleman who knew my grandparents. I explained I had never known my grandfather and asked if he had any information about him. Reverend Cook promised to check his files, and, to my delight, sent me a large fat envelope two week later. The envelope contained minutes of state conventions where my granddad had presided, sermons he had preached, and many other references to family members. However, the most precious document he sent was a yellowed, dog-eared essay entitled, "The Testimony of Sister E. C. Rider."

My grandmother's words thrilled and completely captivated me as she wrote how she and my grandfather found Christ in 1917. After feeling a call to the ministry, they sold all their possessions and lived by faith. She told of God's miraculous provision, protection in the face of grave danger, and how they had devoured God's Word, even though the only Bible they owned had a considerable portion missing.

Could it have been my grandparents' prayers that drew me into the Kingdom despite the lack of the Christian environment in my home? Were they the reason we saw my mother, father, and my uncles come to Christ one by one?

Discovering my Christian roots meant more to me than I could have imagined. It was the *best* gift.

Jesus, we know the gifts received from Your hand are always good—even perfect. Thank You for meeting the deepest needs of our souls. Amen.

Shirley Rose uses her own gifts to help other women through her writing, speaking, and Emmy-nominated television program, *Aspiring Women.*

Prayer Walking

Janet Holm McHenry

Pray without ceasing.

1 Thessalonians 5:17 NASB

About four years ago I was a physical mess. I was overweight, tired all the time, and couldn't get to sleep without painkillers—my hips hurt so bad. The climactic moment hit when my knees gave way as I walked down our back steps one day. I determined right then and there to get back into shape, so the next morning I got up a little earlier and started walking.

I knew God also wanted me to begin a deeper prayer life, so I decided to pray while I walked. I've been prayer walking ever since. Eventually God showed me that He wanted me to pray for whatever I saw along my path, and soon I found that I was praying even when I wasn't walking. I had begun to see that wherever God had me during my day was my prayer territory, so to speak. My purpose is to make a difference for Him wherever I am—and that begins with prayer.

I began to understand what Paul meant when he wrote, *"Pray without ceasing."* When I read the newspaper as I come back in from walking, I pray for the needs around my world. When I go into my English classroom at the high school where I teach, I pray for my students and fellow teachers, as God leads me. As I'm standing in the bank line behind a young mom with a cranky baby, I pray for her.

I've found a whole new purpose for my life as a result of taking my prayer walk right into and through the rest of my day. And I've changed too—all those physical symptoms are gone, as well as depression and fear that used to manipulate my days. Praying without ceasing: I've found it's a whole new outlook on life!

Lord, thank You for Your directive to pray without ceasing, for it keeps us focused on You during our day, rather than on ourselves. Show me how to pray today. Amen!

Janet Holm McHenry has authored two books on prayer walking, *PrayerWalk* and *Daily PrayerWalk*, and now has all kinds of folks from the three churches in her little town walking and praying.

My Job Is To Say, "I Love You"

Carmen Leal

For I am convinced that neither death nor life, neither angels nor demons, neither the present nor the future, nor any powers, neither height nor depth, nor anything else in all creation, will be able to separate us from the love of God that is in Christ Jesus our Lord.

Romans 8:38-39 NIV

Before my husband David entered a nursing home, Huntington's disease had robbed him of his ability to feed himself. One day, with more food landing on his shirt than in his mouth, David and I were going through the usual "change the shirt" game.

His garbled speech made David's response to my urging impossible to comprehend. I did, however, figure out that he had no intention of lifting his arms or cooperating as I changed the shirt.

"David, my job is to feed you, make sure you take your medications, and help your doctors. Your job is to help me to help you. You need to lift your arms, please."

With an endearing smile so like that of the man I married before the ravages of Huntington's disease, David said, "No. My job is to say 'I love you' in as clear a voice as possible."

A few years ago I shared that story with my pastor, Dr. Hunter, and he put his own spin on the anecdote one Sunday from the pulpit. He said, "Isn't that like us? We tell God what His job is and expect Him to do our bidding."

Dr. Hunter went on to explain that God's job isn't to make sure we have enough money or to get everything we want in life. Instead, God says, "No. My job is to say 'I love you' in as clear a voice as possible."

Over the years I've experienced loss and pain, but I've also heard God's sweet voice reminding me, "My job is to say 'I love you' in as clear a voice as possible." He does that every day in a myriad of ways and I know, despite the pain and loss, that nothing will ever separate me from the love of God.

Dear Lord, thank You for telling me clearly how much You love me. Help me to hear Your voice, especially when discouragement and unrest intrude into my life.

Carmen Leal is an author, speaker, and singer. Her mission is, "To help the hurting world accept finite disappointment while accepting the infinite hope of eternal salvation through Jesus Christ."

Cheerful Heart

Martha Bolton

The cheerful heart hath a continual feast.

Proverbs 15:15 NET

If we keep a cheerful heart, we can have joy in both the good times and the bad times, when everything is going right and when everything is going wrong.

The word "continual" means "all the time." No matter what we're going through, we can have this joy. It's not a "little giggle" type of joy. It says that our joy will be a "feast." A feast of joy means belly laughs—uproarious laughter. It is a joy unspeakable both inward and outward. Not that we would laugh at serious problems, but we can certainly laugh our way through them by finding other areas of our life that are laughable.

God knows the importance of humor. That's why He created us with the ability to laugh. He knew we'd need it, so He gave us the equipment. Laughter is healing. It's a good medicine. And when we're going through tough times, it just could be the secret to our survival.

Lord, help me to remember that Your joy is healing,
and it doesn't expire when things get tough.

Martha Bolton is an Emmy- and Dove-nominated writer, the author of fifty books, and has written comedy for Bob Hope, Wayne Newton's USO show, Phyllis Diller, Ann Jillian, John Davidson, Mark Lowry, and Jeff Allen.

Revolutionized

Kathy Collard Miller

There is no fear in love; but perfect love casts out fear.
1 John 4:18 NASB

One afternoon as I drove home from church feeling downhearted, I thought, *Why can't I love God enough?* I was afraid that if I didn't love Him enough, He would never fully accept me as His child. I meditated on 1 John 4:18, and it seemed to scream of my need to have a perfect love toward God: "See, Kathy," I berated myself, "if your love for God was perfect, you wouldn't have any fear of Him."

Then as I stopped the car at a red light, I was struck with a different view of this verse. *Wait a minute, Lord. This verse isn't talking about my love for You, but Your love for me. Now I understand. Your perfect love can cast out my fear because You want only what's best for me. Oh, thank You!*

My thinking was revolutionized. No longer was I required to "love enough." God's unconditional and never-ending love—

His perfect love—could take away my fears and assure me He has only good plans in mind for me. I could be a loving Christian, able to love God and please Him.

Charles Morgan said, "There is no surprise more wonderful than the surprise of being loved; it is God's finger on [our] shoulder."[4] That's how I felt in that moment. I was set free to receive God's unconditional love and to love Him back. Not a love that demanded more and more—a "more" that I can't fulfill—but a love that is satisfied based on Jesus' substitute sacrificial death.

Father God, thank You that You provided a way for me to love You through Your Son, Jesus. I'm so grateful for Your unconditional love that loves me no matter what. Amen.

Kathy Collard Miller is the author of forty-two books including *Through His Eyes*. She is a popular women's conference speaker and has spoken in twenty-five states and four foreign countries.

[4]Sherwood Eliot Wirt and Kersten Beckstom, *Topical Encyclopedia of Living Quotations* (Minneapolis, MN: Bethany House, 1982), 148.

God's Song

Teresa Turner Vining

The LORD your God is with you, he is mighty to save.
He will take great delight in you, he will quiet you
with his love, he will rejoice over you with singing.
Zephaniah 3:17 NIV

It had taken longer than we had hoped, but I was finally pregnant with our first child. Everything seemed to be going well. Then we received a call telling us that one of the tests indicated that our baby might have a debilitating genetic disease.

Suddenly we were faced with the knowledge that our baby might never walk or speak or do any of the other things parents live to see their children do. The only way we could know for sure was to do another test that brought a chance of miscarriage with it, and we didn't want to take that risk.

Those last three months of pregnancy involved much uncertainty and tears. During that time, my aunt, a dedicated intercessor, told me that God had directed her to a specific verse for our child and us. It was Zephaniah 3:17.

I meditated on that verse for the rest of the pregnancy. God can save. He will be our comfort and strength. He rejoices in my husband, our child, and in me so much that He breaks out in song.

On April 27, 1999, our son, Zephan Erik Vining, was born, a perfectly healthy child. I rejoiced that God chose to save. But I knew there would be other hard times, and I purposed to cement this verse in my heart to remind me of God's power, comfort, and head-over-heels love for me.

Lord, thank You that You delight and rejoice in me.
Please teach me to trust in You and Your love always—
regardless of the circumstances. Amen.

Teresa Turner Vining lives in the Kansas City area with her husband and two sons. Her latest book is *Making Your Faith Your Own: A Guidebook for Believers with Questions.*

Daily Renewal

Lael Arrington

Therefore we do not lose heart. Though outwardly we are wasting away, yet inwardly we are being renewed day by day. For our light and momentary troubles are achieving for us an eternal glory that far outweighs them all. So we fix our eyes not on what is seen, but on what is unseen. For . . . what is unseen is eternal.

2 Corinthians 4:16-18 NIV

Some of us are wasting away faster than others. At twenty-nine I was diagnosed with rheumatoid arthritis. My descent from slightly tarnished Beauty Queen to cripple was swift. All my dreams leaked out of my heart, leaving me with barren grief that occasionally trickled down my cheeks as I passed certain signposts—the days I could no longer play my guitar or wear my wedding ring—the little swollen, aching things that stood for the big broken thing.

I've thought about Paul's words, "light and momentary troubles." God, are You taking me seriously!? Daily pain, so many surgeries? I felt like Snow White stuck with the body of the hobbling hag with the apple. Even the "Snow White" was anemia induced.

For years I prayed St. Lael's Prayer of Resignation: "Lord, I know I should be happy with my lot. If this is what You want for me, then give me the grace to settle for it. Amen."

And He did . . . sort of. I lived on the edge of contentment. I did not lose heart. But I certainly would wander off into fantasies of the life I longed for.

My longings grew. My prayers became desperate. *Lord, help! I can't settle!*

"I never wanted you to," He replied.

He stoked my gifts, moved me into teaching. He sat me down to write and showed me the kingdoms of this world, not their splendor, but their brokenness and our need to cast a vision of Kingdom-reality for our families and neighbors.

"I have higher dreams for you," He said. And as I truly fix my eyes on my King and His Kingdom I've come to know His heart and caught a glimpse of eternity, that "city with foundations" where He waits at the finish.

Ah, Lord God, thank You for rescuing my heart,
for replacing my duty with delight. Thank You for the
eternal weight and meaning RA [rheumatoid arthritis]
has added to my life, both now and for eternity.

A pastor's wife and mother of a grown son, Lael Arrington's worldview expertise is woven into *Worldproofing Your Kids, Pilgrim's Progress Today,* and her national speaking ministry.

For Me

Kristy Dykes

"Seek first the kingdom of God and His righteousness, and all these things shall be added to you."
Matthew 6:33 NKJV

Ever since I was a child, Matthew 6:33 has been my guidepost. I was taught, "If you will do right and live right and be right, God will bless you," both at church and at home by a godly mother, who, incidentally, placed fifth in the nation at the 1995 Henrietta Mears' Sunday School Teachers' Contest.

Throughout my life, I have sought God with a sincere heart. "Lord, use me inYour Kingdom however You see fit" is my prayer. In my kaleidoscopic life as a minister's wife, I have sipped tea and swatted flies with the saints; and along the way I have directed choirs, taught Sunday school and children's church, served as youth pastor, led women's groups, played the piano and organ, written/directed/starred in church plays, and cleaned enough commodes to last a lifetime! But I did it all to glorify God and further His Kingdom, putting my own desires aside.

And so when God whispered to me, "I want you to write for Me," I did. I not only wrote and published for periodicals but I also went to school and earned a degree in mass communications/journalism.

But my dream was to write Christian fiction and see it published because I believe in its use in ministry. Matthew 13:34 CEV says, "Jesus used stories when he spoke to the people. In fact, he did not tell them anything without using stories."

"When will this happen?" I asked the Lord.

"Keep putting Me first," He whispered to my heart. And He was right. I learned that when we put God first, He blesses us. I can't wait to see what He will do next!

Heavenly Father, help me to always put You first in my life. Help me to seek after Your ways, not my ways. And as I do this, I know that You will bless me indeed. Amen.

Kristy Dykes is an award-winning author and speaker. She serves on the publications advisory board of *Woman's Touch* magazine and is a Christian fiction author published in *American Dream* and *Sweet Liberty.*

What the Locusts Have Eaten

J a n   C o l e m a n

I will repay you for the years the locusts have eaten.
Joel 2:25 NIV

Years ago, a green wagon rumbled up my country driveway in a screen of red dust. The geese chased the rear tires trying to jackhammer them with their beaks. *At least something was trying to protect the homestead.*

A woman kicked her booted foot at the geese. She was no stranger to ranch life. At the door, she said, "I'm Joyce. I read your newspaper column every week. Lately, I've had the urge to pray for you. Now I know why. I'm so sorry."

Flabbergasted, I groped for words, but none came, only a mew like the tiny cry of a baby kitten unsure of where to find warmth in the darkness. *The whole community knows my husband left me for another woman, and my young daughter walked out the same door with him.*

We made small talk about my ferocious watch-geese until Joyce said, "I have a Bible for you." She opened the tattered pages to the book of Joel: *I will restore to you the years the locusts have eaten*.

"It's a promise from God to His people," she explained. "He will rebuild your life if you turn to Him."

I identified with an insect invasion—disaster swooping down on my life, turning day into night. And God had an answer for this?

Joyce didn't beat around the bush. She told me, like a gentle prophet, I needed the Lord. My heart pinched at the truth. My own resources were dried up, and I was plagued with regret.

I didn't know how it could happen, but clearly God had sent this bold woman to my door with a message of hope. I couldn't depend on the husband of my youth, but I could trust the God who would never fail me.

Lord, thank You for the mysterious way You restore our ruined dreams, how You never waste a hurt but use them to bring us a spiritual harvest that cannot be destroyed.

Jan is finding deeper meaning for her life *After the Locusts* (title of her first book) as she encourages other women to depend on God's promises.

Index

About the Compilers

Linda Evans Shepherd is a nationally recognized speaker, a member of the National Speakers Association, and an award-winning, prolific author. She speaks to women who want to laugh and draw closer to God and to each other. She has authored several books, including *Teatime for Women*. She has been on countless radio and TV programs from coast to coast. Linda has started a new ministry for Women Who Minister to Women, as well as to advanced women authors and speakers, and a national radio program, Right to the Heart (http://www.righttotheheart.com/).

Married for over twenty years, Linda has two children and is President of Shepherd Heart Productions (http://www.sheppro.com./). Linda writes and speaks to encourage others.

Linda understands how to encourage because she has received encouragement herself. When her daughter, Laura, was 18 months old, she was in a car accident which left her in a ten-month-long coma, with severe handicaps. Through this experience, Linda has learned many deep lessons with God, lessons she now shares with others.

Eva Marie Everson is a nationally recognized speaker and the 2002 AWSA Member of the Year. She has authored several books including a suspense/intrigue trilogy: *Shadow of Dreams*, *Summon the Shadows*, and *Shadows of Light*.

In the summer of 2002, Eva Marie traveled with five other Christian journalists to Israel for a special ten-day press trip that, in turn, changed her life. Upon her return, she authored the highly acclaimed "Falling Into the Bible" series for Crosswalk.com and enrolled in seminary.

Married to Dennis, Eva Marie has four children and three grandchildren. The goal of her ministry is to draw others into a more intimate relationship with God. Eva Marie's website can be found at www.evamarieeverson.com.

About the Advanced Writers and Speakers Association (AWSA)

Advanced Writers and Speakers Association is a professional support group made up of the top 10 percent of Christian women in both publishing and speaking. Currently, we are more than 200-women strong, and we are sponsored by the 501(c) 3 nonprofit ministry of Right To The Heart.

Our main event is the annual AWSA conference which is held just prior to the opening of the CBA (Christian Booksellers' Trade Show). We also sponsor prayer teleconferences, prayer retreats, and the Golden Scroll Awards Banquet.

Our communication centers around an online loop where we find connection and prayer support with those who are traveling similar journeys. Our members can choose to be contacted daily or only for special announcements.

Our Golden Scroll Awards Banquet also takes place just prior to the opening of CBA. We invite authors, editors, and publishers to gather for our presentation of the Golden Scroll Member, Editor, and Publisher of the Year Awards.

We are open only to those Christian women communicators who have written at least two books and who speak to groups of 100 at least three times a year across state lines. To join AWSA, fill out our online membership application at the following website:

http://www.righttotheheart.com/women/

Additional copies of this title are available
from your local bookstore.

If you have enjoyed this book, or if it has impacted your life,
we would like to hear from you.

Please contact us at:

Honor Books
An Imprint of Cook Communications Ministries
4050 Lee Vance View
Colorado Springs, CO 89018

Or by e-mail at *cookministries.com*